SAMUEL L. BRENGLE

COME HOLY GUEST

Bob Hostetler, General Editor

wesleyan
PUBLISHING HOUSE
wphstore.com

CREST BOOKS

Copyright © 2016 by The Salvation Army
Published by Wesleyan Publishing House
Indianapolis, Indiana 46250
Printed in the United States of America
ISBN: 978-1-63257-072-7
ISBN (e-book): 978-1-63257-073-4

Library of Congress Cataloging-in-Publication Data

Brengle, Samuel Logan, 1860-1936.
  Come holy guest / Bob Hostetler, general editor.
    pages cm. -- (Samuel L. Brengle's holy life series)
  "This work is a revised combination of the following books: Guest of the Soul
and When the Holy Ghost Is Come."
  ISBN 978-1-63257-072-7 (pbk.)
  1. Holy Spirit. 2. Christianity. I. Hostetler, Bob, 1958- editor. II. Brengle, Samuel
Logan, 1860-1936. Guest of the soul. III. Brengle, Samuel Logan, 1860-1936.
When the Holy Ghost is come. IV. Title.
  BT121.3.B68 2016
  231'.3--dc23
                                    2015030476

Contents

Preface

Samuel Logan Brengle was an influential author, teacher, and preacher on the doctrine of holiness in the late nineteenth to early twentieth century, serving from 1887–1931 as an active officer (minister) in The Salvation Army. In 1889 while he and his wife, Elizabeth Swift Brengle, were serving as corps officers (pastors) in Boston, Massachusetts, a brick thrown by a street "tough" smashed Brengle's head against a door frame and caused an injury severe enough to require more than nineteen months of convalescence. During that treatment and recuperation period, he began writing articles on holiness for The Salvation Army's publication, *The War Cry*, which were later collected and published as a "little red book" under the title *Helps to Holiness*. That book's success led to eight others over the next forty-five years: *Heart Talks on Holiness*, *The Way of Holiness*, *The Soul-Winner's Secret*, *When the Holy Ghost Is Come*, *Love-Slaves*, *Resurrection Life and Power*,

Ancient Prophets and Modern Problems, and *The Guest of the Soul*
(published in his retirement in 1934).

By the time of his death in 1936, Commissioner Brengle was an inter-
nationally renowned preacher and worldwide ambassador of holiness.
His influence continues today, perhaps more than any Salvationist in
history besides the founders, William and Catherine Booth.

I hope that the revised and updated editions of his books that
comprise the Samuel L. Brengle's Holy Life Series will enhance and
enlarge that influence, introduce these writings to new readers, and
create fresh interest in those who already know the godly wisdom and
life-changing power of these volumes.

While I have taken care to preserve the integrity, impact, and voice
of the original writing, I have carefully and prayerfully made changes
that I hope will facilitate greater understanding and appreciation of
Brengle's words for modern readers. These changes include:

- Revising archaic terms (such as the use of King James English) and
  updating the language to reflect more contemporary usage (such as
  occasionally employing more inclusive gender references);
- Shortening and simplifying sentence structure and revising
  punctuation to conform more closely to contemporary practice;
- Explaining specific references of The Salvation Army that will
  not be familiar to the general population;
- Updating Scripture references (when possible retaining the King
  James Version—used exclusively in Brengle's writings—but frequently incorporating modern versions, especially when doing
  so will aid the reader's comprehension and enjoyment);

- Replacing Roman numerals with Arabic numerals and spelled out Scripture references for the sake of those who are less familiar with the Bible;

- Citing Scripture quotes not referenced in the original and noting the sources for quotes, lines from hymns, etc.;

- Aligning all quoted material to the source (Brengle, who often quoted not only Scripture, but also poetry from memory, often quoted loosely in speaking and writing);

- Adding occasional explanatory phrases or endnotes to identify people or events that might not be familiar to modern readers;

- Revising or replacing some chapter titles, and (in *Ancient Prophets and Modern Problems*) moving one chapter to later in the book; and

- Deleting the prefaces that introduced each book and epigraphs that preceded some chapters.

In the preface to Brengle's first book, Commissioner (later General) Bramwell Booth wrote, "This book is intended to help every reader of its pages into the immediate enjoyment of Bible holiness. Its writer is an officer of The Salvation Army who, having a gracious experience of the things whereof he writes, has been signally used of God, both in life and testimony, to the sanctifying of the Lord's people, as well as in the salvation of sinners. I commend him and what he has here written down to every lover of God and His kingdom here on earth."

In the preface to Brengle's last book, *The Guest of the Soul*, The Salvation Army's third general (and successor to Bramwell Booth) wrote: "These choice contributions . . . will, I am sure, serve to strengthen the faith of the readers of this book and impress upon them the joyousness of life when the heart has been opened to the Holy Guest of the Soul."

I hope and pray that this updated version of Brengle's writings will further those aims.

—Bob Hostetler

general editor

PART ONE

Guest of the Soul

The Atonement 1

It was once my joyful privilege to spend five months in intensive and fruitful evangelistic work in Norway in early 1907. Two movements were attracting wide attention in the country. In Oslo, then known as Christiana, what is popularly known as the "tongues movement" was arousing unusual interest—as indeed it was throughout Norway and in other parts of Northern Europe. It was claimed that the apostolic gifts of the Spirit were restored to the church, and many were seeking the baptism of the Holy Spirit with special emphasis placed upon the gift of tongues as the one necessary and invariable sign of the baptism.

At the same time, in Bergen, the second city of the kingdom, the so-called "new theology" had been accepted and preached with eloquence and zeal by one of the most popular and influential state clergymen in the city.[1] Other pastors flew to the faith's defense with learned arguments, which left the man or woman on the street in much perplexity and uncertainty. Since I was to visit Bergen, the local Salvation Army officer (minister), Adjutant Theodor Westergaard,[2] wrote and begged me to speak on the subject, promising to secure the finest hall in the city (the one in which the controversy had begun and been carried on) and to gather a representative audience to hear me.

I have never considered myself so much an advocate as a witness, and I did not wish to begin a few days' revival campaign by getting mixed up in a controversy of which I knew so little, and with a gentleman of whom I knew nothing. However, I wrote the adjutant that, if he wished to advertise me to speak on the atonement from the standpoint of an evangelist and a witness, he might do so. I was then visiting the cities on the south and west coasts of Norway, conducting two, three, and four meetings a day, traveling (poor sailor that I am) on little, comfortless coastal steamers, with no books but my Bible and songbook and no one with whom I could talk over the subject. With almost every waking hour filled with work, and wearied by long and exacting meetings, I could make only a few notes on an envelope I carried in my pocket. But I prayed, meditated, communed with God, sought His inspiration and guidance, thought my way through my subject, and trusted for divine help.

The following is the substance of my address that evening in Bergen, clothed in the language used as nearly as I was able to recall after some weeks in which I was still engaged in exacting labors.[3] It is in no sense an exhaustive study of the atonement. I was in a strange city on the eve of only a few days of evangelistic labors for the salvation and sanctification of souls. The object of the address was not so much to answer critics and to satisfy the demand of scholarship as to reach the hearts of plain men and women with the importance, need, and nature of God's great gift of love and sacrifice in His Son for the redemption of humanity.

I had just one hour and had to speak through an interpreter, who took up half my time. There was no opportunity for elaborate reasoning or to discuss various theories of the atonement. I was able to give only a simple presentation of truth that would win people to Christ and reconcile them to God. During the following eight days' meetings, more than six hundred men, women, and children publicly sought pardon and purity.

No other subject the human mind can consider is so vitally important, so humbling, and yet so ennobling in its effect as the atonement — the work and act of our Lord Jesus Christ in suffering and dying for human souls that He might save them from sin.

It is a subject which leads to the profoundest questions and often to the most perplexing and distressing doubts which cannot be ended by argument nor settled by human learning and skillful reasoning, but only by faith in the records found in the Bible and worked out in experience. Nevertheless, arguments and illustrations may in some measure help our faith and guide our minds to a right understanding of a matter which is either of infinite importance or else of no importance at all.

SIN: WHAT IT IS

Right in the forefront of the discussion we are face-to-face with the great problem of sin. If there is no sin, no evil estrangement from God, then there is no need of an atonement, of a divine sacrifice to save us.

What is sin? Is it only a mild infirmity due to immaturity, which will be outgrown and corrected by age, like many of the faults and ignorances of children? Or is it a malignantly wrong attitude of the will and affections that will never correct itself? Is it a moral disease like measles and whooping cough that we need not seriously fear, and to which we may indeed safely expose our children? Or is it like a hopeless leprosy or cancer, for which there is no known cure?

I once stepped off the train at home and was met with the announcement that my boy had the measles. I was not alarmed, and he soon recovered. But later I visited a leper hospital, and, oh, the horror of it! There were hopeless invalids with their eyes eaten out and their hands and feet eaten away by the awful disease, looking longingly for death to come and give them release. There was no human cure for them.

If sin is something that corresponds not to measles but to leprosy, I can understand how God, if He loves us and is truly interested in us, might make some great sacrifice, some divine interposition to save us. And it is this sacrifice, this interposition, which constitutes the atonement.

But is sin like leprosy—an awful moral corruption, a malignant attitude of the will and the affections, a corruption of the moral nature that corresponds to leprosy? The Bible says it is. But do the Bible and human history and human experience agree?

In our sheltered Christian homes, and under the protection of laws framed in the light of twenty Christian centuries, we are apt to forget or entirely overlook the malignant character of sin. People brought up in homes where the Bible is read and hymns are sung—where the

Ten Commandments are upheld, where a blessing is asked upon the food, and prayers are offered morning and evening—have little conception of the willful devilry into which men and women sink, and they are liable to be led by their own respectability into a false conception of sin.

SIN: AN ACT

What is sin? God says, "Thou shalt not kill" (Ex. 20:13 KJV). Is it sin to kill? An intelligent woman accidentally poisoned a baby in her home. Was it sin? No one who knew her considered it so. It was an awful mistake, and not a sin, for her will and affections were not malignant, and she was one of the chief mourners at the funeral of the baby.

A little five-year-old child was the firstborn pet and darling of the parents, but then another little one was born into the household, and some foolish women—wickedly foolish women—came into that home and said to the little five-year-old, "You are not Mama's baby and darling now. Mama has another baby that she loves." Jealousy was kindled in that little heart, and one day the child went to its mother with blood on its little hands and said, "Now I am Mama's baby, and now Mama will love her darling." Mama flew to the infant, only to find its head battered in with a hammer by the little five-year-old. That was sin—baby sin, but still sin!

Bear with me while we take a glimpse into the dark depths of what God sees—at what grieves and provokes Him, at some symptoms and manifestations of this hateful thing called sin, which stirred His heart of infinite love and pity and holiness to make such sacrifice to save sinners.

At the height of Rome's power and civilization, the emperor murdered his mother, stamped the life out of his wife and unborn child, and lighted the streets of the city with Christians, whom he had covered with pitch and set on fire. That is sin—sin full-grown. That is not spiritual measles. It is moral and spiritual leprosy.

When I was in Switzerland, I was told of a man and woman who threw their newborn child, born out of wedlock, to the pigs. That was sin!

Why are we shocked at the bare recital of such a story? It was a common thing at the height of Greek and Roman civilization to expose children to beasts, and they were expected to destroy the weak baby.

Do you say we have outgrown this? Why has not China outgrown it? A lady missionary from China told me that she asked a Chinese mother whether she had ever killed one of her girl babies. The woman replied, "Yes, several of them." And when the missionary asked how she could find it in her heart to do such a brutal thing, the woman laughed. It is still common in China. One of our Salvation Army officers rescued a deserted baby left to be devoured by dogs. It is not that we have outgrown China, but we have been lifted out of that terrible darkness and brutality by pierced hands. It is the light of the cross shining upon us that has made the approval of such deeds impossible among us.

SIN: A STATE OF HEART

But sin is not merely an act. It is a state of the heart as well. A professing Christian said to me, "There is pride in my heart, and I get angry." And I tried to draw a word picture which would show her the sin of pride and anger.

Here is Jesus in Pilate's judgment hall. They have spat in His face, crowned Him with thorns, stripped Him, tied His hands to His feet, and beaten His bare back till it is bruised and bleeding. They have placed the cross upon His shoulders and, pale and worn with the bitter agony, with the spittle on His face and the blood on His brow, He struggles up the hill under the heavy load.

You come behind Him, and you say, "I am His follower. I am a Christian. I love Him." He is the very essence of lowliness and humility, but you come strutting behind Him in pride—proud of the feather in your hat, the bloom on your cheek, your money in the bank, your home that is better than other people have, your good name, or some gift that lifts you above others. You are proud of these things, and you look down with a certain superciliousness and condescension on others, consider yourself just a little bit better than they, and hold yourself aloof from them, while professing to follow this lowly Cross-Bearer. You have a right to be grateful to Him for those gifts that have lifted you above others but no right to be proud, and your pride is an abomination and sin before Him, a spiritual leprosy which only God can heal.

But He has reached the top of the hill. Hard, rough soldiers have thrown Him down upon the cross, driven the nails through His hands and feet, and, lifting the cross, have set it in its socket with a terrible thud, adding agony to the suffering Victim. And they mock Him, rob Him of His only suit of clothes, and cast dice for His seamless robe. And He prays, "Father, forgive them; for they know not what they do!"

And you stand at the foot of the cross, a professing Christian, His follower. And some man or woman approaches you, and you frown and step aside, for you are angry with that one. In the presence of that compassionate and forgiving Sufferer on the cross, I say that your anger is a sin, which cannot be washed out with rose water. It is moral leprosy. It is a malignant thing, which cannot be washed out with a few tears, but must be purged with blood, the blood of God's dear Son.

SIN: A CRIME AGAINST GOD

But sin is also a crime against God. If I murder a man, I sin against him, his poor wife, and his helpless children. But they do not punish me; the state punishes me. I have sinned against the state and the whole community. I have broken its laws. I have made a breach in the safeguards that secure the people from crime and danger, and that breach can be closed only by my punishment.

Looking at it in this light, we can rise to the vision of sin as a blow against God and His righteous government and the safeguards He has placed around His moral creation. David stole the wife of Uriah the Hittite and secured Uriah's murder but, when self-convicted by the prophet Nathan's story, he saw that he had sinned against God and cried out, "Against you, and you alone, have I sinned; I have done what is evil in your sight" (Ps. 51:4 NLT).

Hundreds of years before, Joseph had been tempted to commit a similar sin. He resisted and overcame the temptation, saying, "How then can I do this great wickedness, and sin against God?" (Gen. 39:9 KJV).

How could those men say that this sin, which in such a peculiar sense is a sin against another human being, was sin against God? Listen! Do you remember Jesus' parable describing the final judgment?

Then the King will say to those on his right, "Come, you who are blessed by my Father, inherit the Kingdom prepared for you from the creation of the world. For I was hungry, and you fed me. I was thirsty, and you gave me a drink. I was a stranger, and you invited me into your home. I was naked, and you gave me clothing. I was sick, and you cared for me. I was in prison, and you visited me."

Then these righteous ones will reply, "Lord, when did we ever see you hungry and feed you? Or thirsty and give you something to drink? Or a stranger and show you hospitality? Or naked and give you clothing? When did we ever see you sick or in prison and visit you?"

And the King will say, "I tell you the truth, when you did it to one of the least of these my brothers and sisters, you were doing it to me!"

Then the King will turn to those on the left and say, "Away with you, you cursed ones, into the eternal fire prepared for the devil and his demons. For I was hungry, and you didn't feed me. I was thirsty, and you didn't give me a drink. I was a stranger, and you didn't invite me into your home. I was naked, and you didn't give me clothing. I was sick and in prison, and you didn't visit me."

Then they will reply, "Lord, when did we ever see you hungry or thirsty or a stranger or naked or sick or in prison, and not help you?"

And he will answer, "I tell you the truth, when you refused to help the least of these my brothers and sisters, you were refusing to help me."

And they will go away into eternal punishment, but the righteous will go into eternal life. (Matt. 25:34–46 NLT)

And what meaning has the parable but this: that the King so identifies Himself with every needy and suffering subject in His vast domain that neglect of or a blow against that subject is counted by the King as a sin against Himself? It is God's law that is broken. It is God's authority that is defied. It is God's holiness and justice that are despised. When a man or woman sins, it is against God.

Indeed, sin is nothing less than lawlessness—a huge selfishness—that amounts to moral and spiritual anarchy. We sinners would pull God off His throne and kill Him if we could. I was not a bad boy as people count badness, but I can remember how, in my childish pride and vaulting ambition, I wondered why I should be a creature subordinated to God and subject to His righteous and unfailing judgments, and I disliked Him and wished I could pull Him off His throne and seat myself upon it, so that I might be responsible to no one but myself. And does not Jesus teach in His parable of the householder that this is the character of sin?

Now listen to another story. A certain landowner planted a vineyard, built a wall around it, dug a pit for pressing out the grape juice, and built a lookout tower. Then he leased the vineyard to tenant farmers and moved to another country. At the time of the grape harvest, he sent his servants to collect his share of the crop. But the farmers grabbed his servants, beat one, killed one, and stoned another. So the landowner sent a larger group of his servants to collect for him, but the results were the same.

Finally, the owner sent his son, thinking, "Surely they will respect my son."

But when the tenant farmers saw his son coming, they said to one another, "Here comes the heir to this estate. Come on, let's kill him and get the estate for ourselves!" So they grabbed him, dragged him out of the vineyard, and murdered him. (Matt. 21:33–39 NLT)

What does Jesus teach here but that sin is a state of heart rebellion that, carried to its final issues, would rob and kill God Himself if that were possible? We sinners want to have our own way and gratify our own desires and pleasures, regardless of the glory of God and the highest good of others. In reality, we want to be a law unto ourselves. We want to be our own God.

Sin can fawn and appear innocent and fair to behold, but it is utterly false and cruel. There are men and women, possibly in your neighborhood, who would not hesitate an instant to rob you, if they could, of your last penny and leave you a homeless beggar. They would not hesitate a moment to debauch your innocent boy, your lovely daughter, your sweet sister, and sink them to the lowest depths of infamy, and then glory in their shame. How little do we know the awful depths and darkness of sin—the corruption, iniquities, wickednesses, vile affections, lusts, and vaulting ambitions into which sin leads men and women! And what will God do with a hateful thing like this? What attitude must God take toward sin?

SIN: A CONCERN OF GOD

1. God cannot be ignorant of sin.

2. God cannot be indifferent to sin. It cannot be said of Him, as it was of Gallio, that He "cared for none of those things" (Acts 18:17 KJV).

3. God cannot approve sin, for then He would be the chief of sinners.

4. God must be utterly and totally antagonistic to sin, and He must do so with all the strength of His great moral being.

He must hate and condemn sin. Frederick W. Robertson, the great preacher, when he heard of a so-called gentleman plotting the ruin of a beautiful, innocent girl, ground his teeth and clenched his fists in hot indignation. If a righteous man feels that way in the presence of sin, how must a holy God feel? If God does not hate sin, He is not holy. If He does not condemn sin, He is not righteous. If He is not prepared to punish sin, He is not just. But God is holy, righteous, and just. His great heart demands—and His holiness calls for—the utter condemnation of sin. But while God is holy and hates sin with a perfect hatred, yet God is love, and while His holiness demands the punishment and utter destruction of sin, His great heart of love calls for the salvation of the sinner.

SIN: A PROBLEM FOR GOD

How shall God accomplish this double and seemingly contradictory demand of His holy and loving heart? How shall God's love and holiness harmonize to secure mercy for the sinner and judgment against the sin? How can God be just and yet justify the ungodly? How can God look upon sin and justify an ungodly man or woman and yet be a holy God? If a judge on the bench is careless in dealing with criminals or a magistrate winks at crime, they are dangerous people. The judge or magistrate who does not watch over the interests of society and deal hardly and severely with wrongdoing is a dangerous character. And is it not exactly the same with God? How shall God deal with this matter of sin? How shall His great heart of love secure its end—the salvation of the soul—and His great heart of holiness secure its end—the condemnation of sin? How shall God justify the ungodly and yet Himself be just?

Here is a problem for God: Fools mock at sin, but God does not. Foolish men and women think it is a very simple problem, this matter of the forgiveness of sins. But it is the profoundest problem in the moral universe, one which no other religion save the Christian faith has been able to solve—and in its solution lie our hope and our peace.

Suppose a man commits many crimes—and adds to them rebellion and murder—and is cast into prison. His friends appeal to the ruler to forgive him, and they think it an easy and a simple thing for him to do. But can the ruler do it? He has the authority, but can he do it and be just and safeguard his people? There are many things he must consider:

1. Would it not harm the man himself to pardon him, if he were not truly repentant?

2. Would it not encourage evil men and women in wickedness, and that possibly in far distant parts of the ruler's dominion?

3. Would it not endanger society and dismay good people by sweeping away the safeguards of law and order and by ignoring, if not destroying, the distinction between well-doing and wrongdoing?

God is confronted with a problem like this. How do we know, when we talk lightly about God's mercy, what other worlds are looking on to see how God will deal with sin in this world? Children watch to see how the wrongdoer will be treated, and nothing will encourage them more quickly to walk in evil ways than to see the wrongdoer smiled and fawned upon.

Parents who have several children know how very careful they must be in dealing with a wrongdoer. Their hearts may feel very tender toward the little one who has done wrong, and their hearts may be breaking with desire to save him or her from punishment. But that child's future and highest good must be placed first, and the other children must not be allowed to think it a light thing to do wrong. There are two ways of ruining children—the way of the harsh father and the way of the indulgent mother. Too much indulgence and too great severity alike will ruin the children. Blessed are the children whose parents know how to keep an even balance between their desire for their children's pleasure and happiness and the necessity of being firm and unbending in the presence of wrongdoing.

To hold an even balance between goodness and severity is divine. "Behold therefore the goodness and severity of God," said Paul (Rom. 11:22 KJV). God is faced with the same kind of problem as we are. How can He at the same time be merciful and just and yet secure the well-being of all His vast dominions? If God pardons sinners before they are penitent, He will only do them harm.

SIN: HOW CAN GOD FORGIVE IT?

How then can God forgive sin and be just?

1. He must secure a true spirit of repentance in the sinful soul or the person whom He forgives will only be hardened in sin.

2. He must make all wrongdoers to know that they cannot sin with impunity in His vast empire.

3. He must safeguard all other moral beings. He must make them feel the holiness of the law and the righteousness of His judgments, until they cry out, "Just and true are your ways, O King of the nations. . . . Yes, O Lord God, the Almighty, your judgments are true and just" (Rev. 15:3; 16:7 NLT).

How can He do this? I think we can make it plain by a simple illustration. Our own relations with one another—parents with children and rulers with their subjects—reflect in some measure the relations of God with us and the problems with which God is confronted in that relationship.

A great teacher who was also a student of human nature once had under his care a boy who was a ringleader in wrongdoing. The boy had been punished before, but broke the rules again and again most flagrantly. One day he committed a more than usually grave offence and was called up for punishment. The punishment was to be two or three sharp raps with a cane on his open palm.

The boy had been punished before, but seemed to enjoy breaking the rules of the school and causing trouble. The teacher knew that he could not allow this to continue. But he was greatly perplexed. He did not want to cast the boy out of the school. He loved the boy and longed to bless and save him, but how could he make him see and understand? How could he let the child go free and at the same time make the other children feel that it was not a slight thing to break the rules of the school?

He stood there with an aching heart in the presence of the defiant boy, when all at once a happy inspiration came to him. He said something like this to the boy: "I don't wish to punish you, but when law is broken somebody must suffer. It is always so, not only in school but out of school as well. So instead of punishing you today, you shall punish me. I will suffer for you."

The boy looked at him and grew crimson. "Give me the punishment," continued the teacher. The boy looked as if he were in a bath of fire. His heart began to melt under a manifestation of love such as he had never witnessed or heard of before. The teacher stretched forth his open hand and said, "Strike!" After long hesitation the poor little fellow nerved himself and struck one blow. And then his proud, rebellious heart broke. He burst into penitential tears, and from that day he became a new creature.

The teacher never had any more trouble with that boy, while the other children felt that it was not a light thing to break the rules of the school. The teacher had found a way to justify a disobedient child and yet make wrongdoing look hateful in the eyes of every other child. He himself suffered, "the just for the unjust" (1 Pet. 3:18 KJV).

An ancient king passed a law against a certain grave crime. The punishment was to be the loss of both eyes. The first criminal discovered was the king's own son. And now what would the king do? How could he save his son and uphold the law throughout his dominion, and compel his subjects to revere him and admire his justice? How could justice and mercy be wedded? The king had said that two eyes must be put out. Could they not be the eyes of a slave? If so, his subjects might fear, but not revere, the king. They would despise him, and the son would go on in his shameless career.

This is what the king did. He put out one of his son's eyes and put out one of his own eyes, and the people could only exclaim, "The king is merciful, and the king is just." He had found a way to save his son and at the same time to uphold the law.

THE ATONEMENT: GOD'S GRACIOUS SOLUTION

Will God act so? Will God suffer to save the sinner? Is there any other way by which God can justify the sinful human soul and yet Himself be just? Is there any other way by which God can display His hatred of sin and His pitying love of the sinner? Is there any other way by which God can break the sinner's proud and unbelieving heart and melt it into penitence and contrition? Is there any other way by which God can retain the respect and confidence of unfallen angels when He pardons sinners and treats them as though they had not sinned? Will God suffer for me? Will He take my place and in His love and pity die in my stead to save me from my sin and its dire consequences?

The Bible says that God will suffer, and that God has suffered. This is the atonement: God's act of condescension and mercy, which bridges the gulf between sinful humans and the holy God; between a wicked, fallen creature and an offended Creator; between a willful and defiant child and a wounded, grieved, and loving Father.

JESUS CHRIST: WHO IS HE?

But when and where did God suffer for me? On Calvary!

But was that dying man on Calvary God? He was the God-man, the Son of God, God the Son (see John 1:1–14; 1 Tim. 3:16).

How can we know God, and where can we find Him? The heaven of heavens cannot contain Him. We cannot see Him. We cannot by searching find Him, but He has focused Himself, as it were, in Jesus Christ. He has humbled Himself to our flesh and blood and stooped to take our nature upon Himself (see Phil. 2:5–8; Heb. 2:14, 16).

The Bible says, "In the beginning was the Word, and the Word was with God, and the Word was God. . . . The Word was made flesh, and dwelt among us . . . full of grace and truth" (John 1:1, 14 KJV). The Bible says He was God.

The apostle Paul told early church leaders, "Shepherd the church of God which He purchased with His own blood" (Acts 20:28 NKJV). So that Sufferer hanging there was God, suffering for us—God, the blessed Son. Wonder of wonders! Think of Him pouring out His life, an innocent Sufferer for sinful men and women, for you and me! "God was in Christ, reconciling the world to himself" (2 Cor. 5:19 NLT), and "in all their suffering he also suffered" (Isa. 63:9 NLT).

The Father's heart of love was pierced with pain by the thorns that pierced the head of the Son. The Father's heart was hurt with the nails that pierced the hands and feet of the Son. The Father's heart was thrust through with anguish at the guilt and sins of men and women when they thrust the spear into the heart of Jesus. The Father suffered with and in the blessed Son.

The whole Trinity is involved in the atoning work of Jesus Christ on Calvary. The Father "so loved the world, that he gave his only begotten Son" (John 3:16 KJV). "God made Christ, who never sinned, to be the offering for our sin, so that we could be made right with God through Christ" (2 Cor. 5:21 NLT). And it was "through the eternal Spirit" that Christ "offered himself without spot to God" (Heb. 9:14 KJV) in our place and on our behalf. Truly did Paul say, "Great is the mystery of godliness: God was manifested in the flesh" (1 Tim. 3:16 NKJV).

The Bible says that Jesus is God. Jesus said so; John said so; Paul said so. The church in all its creeds says so. The wisest Christian teachers say so. The saints and martyrs, who have perished by flame and wild beast's fang, say so. The great soul-winners say so. The humble penitents, rejoicing in the assurance of sins forgiven, say so. And with commingling tears and smiles and heaven-lit faces, they cry out with Thomas, "My LORD and my God!" (John 20:28 KJV).

But the testimonies of the Bible and the creeds and the martyrs and the saints and the soul-winners and the rejoicing penitents do not make me to know that Jesus is Lord, and I may still doubt. How shall I know? May I know? Someone who was born blind may hear a thousand testimonies to the beauties of the starry heavens and the glories of sunrise and sunset and yet doubt them all. It is all hearsay. Is there any way to destroy the doubts forever? Only one, and that is to bestow sight. Then that person will doubt no more. He or she knows and sees firsthand.

An astronomer writes a booklet announcing the discovery of a new star. I may read the booklet and yet may doubt. What shall I do? Throw the booklet away and sit down and write a bigger book than that, to prove that there is no such star and that the astronomer is star-mad or a liar? No, instead let me turn my telescope to that point in the heavens where the new star was reportedly found and find a star mirrored in my telescope! But what if I am mistaken? Then let another, or two, or a thousand people in different parts of the earth turn their telescopes to that point in the heavens. And if they, too, unanimously say, "There is a star," how can I doubt any longer?

JESUS: THE INWARD REVELATION

How can we know that Jesus is Lord? Paul said, "No one can say Jesus is Lord, except by the Holy Spirit" (1 Cor. 12:3 NLT). The Holy Spirit must reveal Him to each heart before doubts about His person can be destroyed. The Bible is the book on divine astronomy that tells when and where to discover Him, "the Bright and Morning Star" (Rev. 22:16 NKJV). It does not reveal Him any more than the book on astronomy reveals the stars. It is only a record of self-revelation, and it tells us how to secure a revelation of Him to our own hearts.

Let us, then, carefully read the instructions in the Bible, the textbook on this heavenly astronomy. Let us look with the eye of faith through the telescope of God's Word, and by true repentance and obedient faith put our souls into that attitude which will enable Him to reveal Himself to us. Let us do what He tells us to do without murmuring and complaining, and then, as myriad others before us have done, we shall find Him formed within our hearts, "the hope of glory" (Col. 1:27 KJV). Our doubts will vanish; our sins will be forgiven; our guilt will be put away. We shall be born again, born of the Spirit. We shall have our eyes anointed with spiritual salve and have our hearts made pure to see God and discover who Jesus is. Then the atonement, made by the shedding of His blood, will no longer be an offense to our imperfect reason and a stone of stumbling to our unbelief; it will be the supreme evidence of God's wisdom and love to our wondering and adoring hearts.

It was this inward and spiritual revelation of Christ that gave Paul such assurance and power. He said, "I know whom I have believed" (2 Tim. 1:12 KJV); "It pleased God . . . to reveal his Son in me" (Gal. 1:15–16 KJV); and "It is no longer I who live, but Christ lives in me" (Gal. 2:20 NLT).

Oh, the joy and infinite peace and satisfaction contained in this spiritual manifestation of Jesus to the heart! It is a fulfillment of those wonderful words of Jesus: "I will come to you. . . . In that day you will know that I am in my Father, and you in me, and I in you. . . . I will . . . manifest myself to [you]" (John 14:18, 20–21 ESV).

I sat beside a student when Christ was manifested to him and saw his face shining almost like the face of an angel. I heard him whisper, "Blessed Jesus! Blessed Jesus!" Later I heard him saying over and over again and again, "Glory be to Jesus! Glory be to Jesus!"

I knelt beside a young lady in prayer, when all at once she burst into tears and cried out in joy, "O Jesus!" He had come, and she knew Him as Lord. Six months later she said, "I'm going to Africa," and with Christ in her heart she went joyfully as a missionary to darkest Africa, where she lived and labored and loved, until one day He said, "It is enough, come up higher," and she went to heaven by way of Africa.

A great businessman found Jesus and with radiant face and deepest reverence said, "I was so mixed up with Jesus that for several days I hardly knew whether it was Jesus or I."

A timid little boy, who was afraid to be left alone in the dark, had the great inward revelation and said quietly and joyfully, "I'm not afraid now, for Jesus is with me."

JESUS: THE GREAT UNVEILING

Who, then, is Jesus Christ? Listen to Isaiah: "For a child is born to us, a son is given to us. The government will rest on his shoulders. And he will be called: Wonderful Counselor, Mighty God, Everlasting Father, Prince of Peace. His government and its peace will never end" (Isa. 9:6–7 NLT).

We look into the Bethlehem manger, and we see only a Child, a little Son, and we are indifferent, though wise men and angels welcome and worship Him with reverent awe and wonder. But little by little, overcome by the insurrection of our passions and tempers and led captive by sin, finding no help in ourselves and proving that "all human help is useless" (Ps. 60:11; 108:12 NLT), we look again and see that He is our help and that "the government will rest on his shoulders" (Isa. 9:6 NLT). And repenting with brokenness of heart and believing in Him, we find pardon and victory and peace as we look. And when the impurity of our nature is more fully revealed, we find instant cleansing in His blood and sanctification full and free in His baptism with the Holy Spirit, and we cry out, "Wonderful!"

Or we are filled with perplexity. Life is a labyrinth, the universe is a riddle, and we walk in a maze. We are at our wits' end. Sages and philosophers cannot answer our anxious questions about the mystery of life; none can solve the problems of triumphant evil and thwarted goodness, of pain and sorrow and loss and death. And again we look and discover that in Him "are hid all the treasures of wisdom and knowledge" (Col. 2:3 KJV). He answers our questions. He resolves our riddles. We rest in Him as our Counselor.

Or we are oppressed with our utter littleness and weakness. We feel as helpless as an insect in the presence of the giant forces of the material universe. We are powerless to resist the vast world movements, the strikes, the conspiracies, the wars, and the political and social upheavals. And in our horror and despair we look again, and see Him in the earthquake and tempest, "towering o'er the wrecks of time,"[4] stilling the storm, raising the dead, calming the fierce and wild passions of humanity, and slowly but surely enlightening and molding the nations. And we cry out, "Mighty God!"

Or we are bereft and lonely and heart-sore. We cry like an orphaned child in the night. There is none to help, and no one understands. Then He draws nigh with infinite comprehension of our heartache and weariness and pain, and with fathomless consolations He folds us in the embrace of His love. We pillow our heads and our hearts on His bosom, nestle close, and whisper, "Everlasting Father, Prince of Peace!"

JESUS: THE ETERNITY OF OUR LORD

Again, we strain our eyes, peering into the future, wondering what its issues will be and what it holds for us and ours. Our loved ones and friends die and pass out of our sight. Life weakens, its full tides ebb, the sun is setting, the night is falling, and we stand by a silent, shoreless sea where we look in vain for a returning sail and upon which we must launch alone. And we cling to life and shrink back with fear. And then He comes walking on the waters and says, "Don't be afraid. I am here!" (John 6:20 NLT). And we are comforted with a great assurance that nothing shall separate us from His love, that He is Lord of life and death, of time and eternity, and that "His government and its peace will never end" (Isa. 9:6–7 NLT).

This is Jesus. We saw Him first as a little babe, a helpless child, on the bosom of a virgin mother, in a stable among the cattle. But oh, how He has grown as we have looked! He "inhabits eternity" (Isa. 57:15 ESV). "The heaven and heaven of heavens cannot contain [Him]" (1 Kings 8:27 KJV). But He stooped to our lowly condition and humbled Himself, suffered and died for us, and made atonement for our sins.

And "how shall we escape, if we neglect so great salvation?" (Heb. 2:3 KJV).

> Oh, the bitter shame and sorrow,
> That a time could ever be
> When I let the Savior's pity
> Plead in vain, and proudly answered:
> "All of self and none of Thee!"
> Yet He found me; I beheld Him
> Bleeding on the cursed tree,
> Heard Him pray, "Forgive them, Father,"
> And my wistful heart said faintly:
> "Some of self and some of Thee!"
> Day by day His tender mercy,
> Healing, helping, full and free,
> Sweet and strong, and, ah! So patient,
> Brought me lower, while I whispered:

"Less of self and more of Thee!"
Higher than the highest heavens,
Deeper than the deepest sea,
Lord, Thy love at last has conquered,
Grant me now my spirit's longing—
"None of self and all of Thee!"[5]

I once heard General William Booth, founder of The Salvation Army, while in the midst of an impassioned appeal for people to repent and make their peace with God, cry out, "Every sinner must be either pardoned or punished." And ever since, those words have remained in my memory as the expression of a tremendous truth from which there is no escape.

As I have written elsewhere:

The atonement opens wide the door of pardon, uttermost salvation, and bliss eternal to every penitent soul who will believe on Christ and follow Him, while it sweeps away every excuse from the impenitent heart that will not trust and obey Him.

The atonement justifies God in all His ways with sinful men and women.

The holiest beings in the universe can never feel that God is indifferent to sin, when He pardons believing souls, lifts up their drooping heads, and introduces them to the glories and blessedness of heaven, because Christ has died for them. On the other hand, the souls who are lost and banished to outer darkness cannot blame God nor charge Him with indifference to their misery, since Christ, by tasting death for them, flung wide open the gateway of escape. That they definitely refused to enter in will be clear in their memory forever and will leave them without excuse.[6]

"Judas went to his own place," the Bible says (Acts 1:25, paraphrase). Now, I ask again, "How shall we escape, if we neglect so great salvation?" (Heb. 2:3 KJV).

Was it for me, for me He died?
And shall I still reject His plea?
Mercy refuse with foolish pride,
The while His heart still yearns for me?
Shall I my cup of guilt thus fill?
While Jesus pleads and loves me still?
Dear Savior, I can ne'er repay
The debt of love I owe!
Here, Lord, I give myself away,
'Tis all that I can do.[7]

NOTES

1. The Church of Norway was at this time an officially recognized, state-funded church of Lutheran background.

2. Theodor Westergaard later became colonel in The Salvation Army.

3. For a detailed description of the meeting, which proved historic, see Clarence W. Hall, *Samuel L. Brengle: Portrait of a Prophet* (New York: The Salvation Army, 1933), 172–181.

4. John Bowring, "In the Cross of Christ I Glory," 1825, public domain.

5. Theodore Monod, "None of Self and All of Thee," 1875, public domain.

6. Samuel L. Brengle, *Love Slaves* (New York: The Salvation Army, 1923), ch. 3.

7. Source unknown.

The Blessedness of the Pentecostal Experience 2

Pentecost was the first great event in the history of Christianity after the ascension of Jesus. It was the fulfillment of Joel's prophecy and Jesus' promise. Joel, hundreds of years before, had prophesied: "Then, after doing all those things, I will pour out my Spirit upon all people. Your sons and daughters will prophesy. Your old men will dream dreams, and your young men will see visions. In those days I will pour out my Spirit even on servants—men and women alike" (Joel 2:28–29 NLT).

And Jesus Himself had promised that if He went away He would send another Comforter or Helper, who would be with them evermore: "Once when he was eating with them, he commanded them, 'Do not leave Jerusalem until the Father sends you the gift he promised, as I told you before. John baptized with water, but in just a few days you will be baptized with the Holy Spirit'" (Acts 1:4–5 NLT).

On the day of Pentecost came the ample fulfillment. They were all filled with the Holy Spirit. That was the final and all-sufficient evidence that Jesus had not been swallowed up and lost in the cloud that had received Him out of their sight but that He had gone home to heaven, that He was upon His throne, and that in His exaltation and exultation He had not forgotten them. They were still in His thoughts and in His love. He was still depending upon them and equipping them with power to carry on His work and fulfill His purpose.

They were exultant. Their joy overflowed. They shined and they shouted. Their hearts caught fire. Their minds kindled into flame. Their tongues were unloosed. They must testify. They trooped downstairs from the upper room and out into the street. This was no mere drawing-room blessing they had received. It was too big, glorious, and good to be confined. They must tell it abroad.

The city of Jerusalem was full of strangers from all parts of the world who had come to the great feast, and to these strangers in their own language the glorious news was told. The populous city was stirred, there was a rush together of the curious multitude, and they were confounded and amazed. They marveled, as each heard the apostles speak in his or her own language. In their amazement and doubt they exclaimed, "What can this mean?" (Acts 2:12 NLT). And well they might. It meant that God had come to tabernacle in the hearts of men and women, and that all heaven was enlisted in a campaign for the salvation of the world, a campaign that would not cease till the earth was "filled with the knowledge of the glory of the LORD, as the waters cover the sea" (Hab. 2:14 KJV).

But some mocked and said, "They're just drunk" (Acts 2:13 NLT). And so they were—drunk with holy joy, gladness, love, quenchless hope, and life eternal.

Peter said, "What you see was predicted long ago by the prophet Joel" (Acts 2:16 NLT), and so it was. The other Comforter had come, and the great days of the church were inaugurated with a mighty revival, in the first meeting of which three thousand people experienced new life through faith in Christ. And every revival from then until now—whether local, in some little church or Salvation Army hall or mission station, or worldwide in its sweep like the Wesleyan revival or that led by William Booth—has flowed from the presence and activities of the Holy Spirit as He has been received in trusting hearts and honored in faith and service.

All lovers of Jesus should in these days seek fresh renewings and a greater fullness of the Holy Spirit. We should study what the Bible says about Him as a person. He is not a mere influence, passing over us like a wind or warming us like a fire. He is a person, seeking entrance into our hearts that He may comfort us, instruct us, empower us, guide us, give us heavenly wisdom, and fit us for holy and triumphant service.

If we will seek His presence and yield ourselves to Him in secret prayer, He will make the Bible a new book to us. He will make Jesus precious to us. He will make God the Father ever real to us. We shall not walk in darkness, but shall have the light of life. We shall not be weak in the presence of duty or temptation, but "strong in the Lord and in his mighty power" (Eph. 6:10 NLT). We shall be "ready for every good work" (Titus 3:1 ESV).

I suggest to all my readers that by way of preparation they prayerfully and carefully study what Jesus said of the Holy Spirit, "the Comforter," in John 14–16, and the Acts of the apostles, which in many respects might be called the Acts of the Holy Spirit, be read and reread again and again, and pondered in faith and prayer.

God has greater things for us and all His people than the world has ever yet seen, if we only believe in the Lord Jesus Christ and permit the Spirit to lead us.

The Bible says, "As many as are led by the Spirit of God, they are the sons of God. . . . And if children, then heirs; heirs of God, and joint-heirs with Christ" (Rom. 8:14, 17 KJV). And heirs can draw on the estate for all those things needed for their well-being and the full development and use of their powers.

The blessing of the Spirit is not given to everybody. Jesus spoke of Him as one "whom the world cannot receive, because it neither sees him nor knows him" (John 14:17 ESV). Jesus did not say, "may not receive," but "cannot receive." He is given only to those who can receive, to those who see and know. A person who has eyes closed to the light, a heart turned from true knowledge, cannot receive. And yet such people are responsible for their own deprivation because their blindness is due to their own action. Such people cannot receive the Holy Spirit because they have turned away from the Savior and the truth that alone could fit them to receive Him.

The Holy Spirit is given only to those who, accepting Christ and following Him, are prepared to receive. The Pentecostal baptism is for an inner circle. It is a family affair. It is for the children who have become sons and daughters of God through penitent, obedient faith.

It is part of their heritage. It is the portion of that immeasurable inheritance in Christ that is bestowed upon them while upon earth. What the measure of that full inheritance will be in the heavenly world no tongue can tell and no heart can conceive. Pentecost is the foretaste. It is that which, received and properly, wisely, diligently used, will fit us for the final and full reward, but which, rejected or neglected, will leave us eternal paupers among those who weep and gnash their teeth in outer darkness.

This Pentecostal blessing is for our comfort while we are away from home and the unveiled presence of the Father. "I will not leave you comfortless," said Jesus, "I will come to you" (John 14:18 KJV). The coming of the Comforter is also the coming of Jesus in the Spirit. Where the Spirit is, there Jesus is. When He is come, we are no longer orphans, lonely and bereft. Though unseen, He is present with us, and our hearts are strangely warmed and comforted. To some of us, this world would be desolate and lonely beyond words if it were not for the presence of the Comforter.

The Pentecostal blessing is for our instruction in the things of God. The Holy Spirit is the great, secret, silent, inward Teacher, speaking to the ears of the soul, whispering in the silences of the night, instructing in the hours of prayer and communion. As Jesus said, "But the Helper, the Holy Spirit, whom the Father will send in my name, he will teach you all things and bring to your remembrance all that I have said to you" (John 14:26 ESV). We are dull and ignorant, making no assured progress in the school of Christ, until the Comforter is come. When He comes, He arouses and quickens our dull minds. He opens wide the closed eyes and the sealed ears of the soul, and we see and hear things that were hidden from us. He brings our inner life into harmony with the mind of God as revealed in the Bible, and its spiritual meaning begins to open up to our understanding. He quickens our memory, and we now can remember the Word of the Lord. We can go home from a meeting and tell what we have heard when the Comforter is in our hearts.

The Pentecostal blessing is for our guidance. There is one way that is everlasting. "Lead me along the path of everlasting life," prayed the psalmist (Ps. 139:24 NLT). There is one—and only one—road that leads home. Heaven is at the end of that way. There are many attractive and alluring byways, but only the one true way, and we need the Comforter to guide us in that way (see John 16:13) and teach us the truth about God, Jesus, salvation and holiness, sin and its consequences, the shed blood that saves from sin, the way of faith and the life of obedience, and the will of God and the joy set before us. It is the way of the cross, of duty, of lowly, humble, faithful service. It is the way of love, truth, justice, and all right and holy living. It is the way of patient well-being, forbearance and kindness, and the spirit that forgives and gives and asks no reward but the grace to give more fully, love more tenderly, believe more firmly, serve more wisely, hope more joyfully, and never to fail.

The Pentecostal blessing is for power. Jesus said, "You will receive power when the Holy Spirit comes upon you" (Acts 1:8 NLT). We are naturally weak. We fall before temptation. We faint with hopelessness, discouragement, or fear in the presence of difficulty or danger. We flame with hasty temper or passion under provocation. We are puffed up with false views of our own ability or importance, or we are cast down by a feeling of our own impotence. But when the Comforter comes, He strengthens us inwardly. He humbles us with a true view of our weakness, our ignorance, our foolishness, and our insufficiency, and then lifts us up with the revelation of God's sufficiency and eagerness to reinforce us at every point of our spiritual need. As Paul wrote, "I fall to my knees and pray to the Father . . . that from his glorious, unlimited resources he will empower you with inner strength through his Spirit" (Eph. 3:14, 16 NLT).

We should watch and pray and trustfully wait—daily, hourly, and moment-by-moment—for that inner strengthening by the Spirit, that we may be strong to work, fight, resist, serve, sacrifice, suffer, dare, bear up, press on joyfully, and not grow weary or fainthearted.

Before Pentecost Peter was ignorant of himself. So conceited was he that he rebuked Jesus for saying that He was to die on a cross, so sure of himself that he boasted that he would die with Jesus, and yet so inwardly weak that when a servant girl pointed him out as one of the disciples, he cursed and swore that he did not know Jesus. But when a few days later the Holy Spirit had come and strengthened Peter inwardly, he boldly preached Christ Jesus to the multitudes in Jerusalem. And when he and John were beaten and threatened and thrown into prison, they gloried that they were counted worthy to suffer and bear shame for Jesus. They were comforted, instructed, guided, and made inwardly strong to do and dare and bear and suffer—by the Pentecostal baptism.

"Sanctification through the Holy Spirit is for power for service!" so many people say. And so it is. It does reinforce and empower the soul. Those who are given over to the Spirit are "endued with power from on high" (Luke 24:49 KJV) and have a spiritual energy and effectiveness that are not of this world. Their lives and their words take on

a strange new influence and power which come from the active cooperation of an unseen guest, a holy and divine presence abiding in love
within them, and this fits them for the service of their Lord.

But service is not the whole purpose of our beings. What we are is
more important than what we do. Goodness is better than greatness. We
may do much and earn a great name and still end in hell. But the person who loves God and others, though unknown beyond a small circle,
is on the way to heaven, and is well-known there. There are those who
are first who shall be last, and those who are last who shall be first.

The Pentecostal blessing is for daily life. The baptism of the Holy
Spirit brings us into union with Christ and into loving fellowship with
the heavenly Father, to fit us snugly into God's great, complex scheme
of life and equip us for such service or sacrifice as falls to our lot. The
busy housewife, the burdened mother, the toiler in mine or factory or
farm or train or ship, the clerk at his or her desk, the merchant prince,
the bootblack and the prime minister, the king and the president, the
schoolboy and girl—all need the Pentecostal blessing for daily life
and duty, as much as any minister or missionary, if they are to live
worthy lives that shall glorify God and do their work in a spirit well
pleasing to Him. We each and all need the blessing of Pentecost, not
simply for service, but for holy, worthy living, for the perfecting and
completing of character from which will flow influences that are often
more effective than the busy activity we call service.

A hardheaded businessman saw a poor widow woman with her
brood of fatherless children going to the house of God Sunday after
Sunday, and one day it convicted him of his sin and neglect and turned
him in repentance and faith to the Savior. Her "patience in well-doing"

(Rom. 2:7 ESV)—which is a fruit of the Spirit—was more effective than any word she could have spoken.

A lawyer came to his wife's pastor and asked to be received as a member of the church. The pastor was glad, for he had preached sermons to reach this man. So he asked, somewhat shamefacedly, which of his sermons had brought him to decision.

"Well, pastor," replied the lawyer, "to tell the truth, it was not one of your sermons. A few Sundays ago I was leaving the church and found old Auntie Blank haltingly trying to get down the icy steps, and I took her arm and helped her. Then she turned her radiant face up to mine, and asked, 'Do you love my Jesus?' It cut to my heart. I saw her peace and overflowing love and joy, in spite of her poverty and rheumatism, and it convicted me of my sin and led me to Christ."

The fruit of the Spirit, manifest in life and look and everyday, unpremeditated speech, often works more silently, deeply, and effectively than our preaching, and only the Pentecostal blessing can produce this fruit to perfection in our lives.

Many years ago I was campaigning in a little city in Minnesota just at the time of the annual meeting of the Methodist Conference. The town was full of Methodist preachers, many of whom attended our Salvation Army open-air meetings, and some of whom came to our hall. Some of them invited me to their testimony meeting on Sunday morning, just before the bishop's great sermon, to give my testimony, which I did. After speaking for some time, I was going to sit down, but they begged me to speak on, so I continued. Then the presiding elder, host of the conference, came in. Seeing me in the pulpit, he peremptorily ordered me to sit down. The preachers protested, while my peace flowed like a river. I assured him I would be through in a moment, and I hurried out to my meeting.

Several of the preachers said, "We have not believed in the blessing, but that Salvationist has it, else instead of smiling and keeping calm and full of peace, he would have taken offense at that presiding elder." They came to our little hall, and in the holiness meeting came to the mercy seat for the blessing. One of them received the fiery, cleansing, humbling baptism and became a witness to the blessing and a flaming evangelist throughout that region.

It was not my preaching, but the fruit of the Spirit that won him. And it was not of me. I am not by nature calm and peaceful. Quite the contrary. It was supernatural. My proud heart had been humbled to receive the Comforter, and graciously and in love He had come. It was He in my heart who kept me peaceful and calm, and to Him be the glory. "Those who love your instructions [and in whom the Comforter abides] have great peace and do not stumble" (Ps. 119:165 NLT). The Pentecostal blessing is given to cleanse and empower the soul and produce such heavenly fruit in earth's harsh climate.

"The Holy Spirit produces this kind of fruit in our lives: love, joy, peace, patience, kindness, goodness, faithfulness, gentleness, and self-control" (Gal. 5:22–23 NLT). And Christians in whom this fruit—full, rich, and ripe—is found have received this Pentecostal blessing and, in spite of infirmities and human frailties and limitations, are reproducing the life of Jesus upon earth. And out of them, most often unconsciously, flow influence and power that are like "rivers of living water" (John 7:38 ESV) in desert lands. In them Christ is magnified (see Phil. 1:20) and the Father is glorified (see John 15:8).

The Guest of the Soul 3

A friend of mine said recently, "I like the term, 'Holy Ghost,' for the word *ghost* in the old Saxon was the same as the word for *guest*." Whether that is so or not, it may certainly be said that the Holy Ghost is the Holy Guest. He has come into the world and visits every heart, seeking admittance as a guest. He may come *to* the soul unbidden, but He will not come *in* unbidden. He may be unwelcome. He may be refused admission and turned away. But He comes. He is in the world like Noah's dove, looking for an abiding place. He comes as a guest, but as an abiding one if received. He forces Himself upon no one. He waits for the open door and the invitation.

He comes gently. He comes in love. He comes on a mission of infinite goodwill, of mercy and peace and helpfulness and joy. He is the Advocate of the Father and of the Son to us humans. He represents and executes the redemptive plans and purposes of the triune God. As my old teacher, Daniel Steele, wrote, "He is the Executive of the Godhead."

When the Holy Spirit comes into a human heart, He convicts of sin. We cease to be self-complacent when He comes. Self-righteousness is seen to be a sheet too short to cover us; our moral and spiritual nakedness is exposed. Our pride is rebuked, and we are ashamed. Our self-conceit vanishes, and we are abashed. Our eyes are opened, and we see how self-deceived we have been—how un-Christlike in our tempers, how corrupt in our desires, how selfish in our ambitions, how puffed up in our vanity, how slow to believe, how quick to excuse ourselves and justify our own ways, how far from God we have wandered, how unfit for heaven we have become.

He thus reveals us to ourselves in love that He may save us, as a wise and good physician shows us our disease in order to get our consent to be cured. But His supreme work of conviction is to convince us how hopelessly we miss the mark because we do not believe and trust in Christ from the heart. This is the sin we do not recognize as sin until He convinces us of it: "The world's sin is that it refuses to believe in me" (John 16:9 NLT).

The Holy Spirit also convicts of righteousness. We no longer justify ourselves and condemn God. Our mouths are stopped. We see that God is true and righteous altogether, and in the presence of His holiness and righteousness, all our righteousness is seen to be as filthy rags. We can only cry, as did the leper, "Lord, if you will, you can make me clean" (Luke 5:12 ESV). And then we see that Christ Jesus was "pierced for our rebellion, crushed for our sins. He was beaten so we could be whole. He was whipped so we could be healed" (Isa. 53:5

NLT), that "He personally carried our sins in his body on the cross so that we can be dead to sin and live for what is right" (1 Pet. 2:24 NLT), that He "suffered for sins, the just for the unjust" (1 Pet. 3:18 KJV), that "God made Christ, who never sinned, to be the offering for our sin, so that we could be made right with God through Christ" (2 Cor. 5:21 NLT), that we might be able joyfully to sing:

> O Love, Thou bottomless abyss,
> My sins are swallowed up in Thee,
> Covered is my unrighteousness,
> Nor spot of guilt remains on me,
> While Jesus' blood, through earth and skies,
> Mercy, free, boundless mercy, cries.[1]

The Holy Spirit convicts of judgment, both now—accompanying our every act, word, thought, intent, and motive, as our shadow accompanies our body—and to come—exact, final, irrevocable, from which there is no escape and no appeal. He convicts of judgment unto life if we are found in Christ, approved of God—life full, complete, eternal and overflowing with bliss, bliss ineffable. And He convicts of judgment unto banishment if we are found out of Christ, disapproved of God—banishment unto outer darkness, banishment eternal, judgment unto woe immeasurable, banishment into shame unutterable, the harvest of our pride, the reaping of our sin. The seed may be small, but the harvest great. From little seeds mighty trees and vast harvests do grow.

When the Holy Ghost becomes the Holy Guest, He opens the eyes of our understanding to understand the Scriptures. Without His aid, the

Bible is just literature, and some of it is dry and hopelessly uninter-
esting and incomprehensible literature. But when He removes the
scales from our eyes and illuminates its pages, it becomes most precious, a new and living Book, in which God speaks to us in love, in
promise, in precept, in types, in symbols, in warning, in rebuke, in
entreaty, and always in love to save. It reveals God. It comforts,
rebukes, inspires, convicts, converts, and rejoices the heart. It is
"sharper than the sharpest two-edged sword," exposing "our inner-
most thoughts and desires" (Heb. 4:12 NLT).

When the Holy Ghost becomes the Holy Guest in the yielded wel-
coming heart, He dwells there un-grieved and with delight. "As the
bridegroom rejoices over the bride" (Isa. 62:5 ESV), so He rejoices
over that soul, while the soul has sweet, ennobling, purifying fellowship and communion with the Lord. He illuminates that soul. He purifies it, sanctifies it, empowers it, instructs it, comforts it, protects it,
adjusts it to all circumstances and crosses, and fits it for effective service, patient suffering, and willing sacrifice.

Some time ago my dear friend of many years, Commissioner
Charles Sowton, who has since gone to heaven, was passing through
New York with his devoted wife. He had only recently settled into his
appointment in Australia, a country he enjoyed, where he felt at home,
and whose people he had come to admire and love, when orders came
to farewell and proceed to England to a new appointment.

To go from sunny Australia to foggy London in midwinter was not
pleasant. To leave a field and work and people he loved for work
where all would be new and strange was not what he expected or
would have chosen. But he told me that the text, "Even Christ didn't

live to please himself" (Rom. 15:3 NLT), kept whispering in his heart, and so with perfect and glad resignation, and in great peace, he and Mrs. Sowton were on their way to their new home and tasks.

As he told me this, his face was as serene as a summer's evening, and my own heart sensed the divine calm that possessed him and was refreshed and blessed. It was the indwelling Holy Guest who whispered those words to his heart and fitted him without murmuring into this providence of God. And He who made him so ready for service and so peaceful in sacrifice.

When the Holy Guest abides within, the soul does not shun the way of the cross, nor seek great things for itself. It is as content to serve in lowly as in lofty ways, in obscure and hidden places as in open and conspicuous places where applause waits. To wash a poor disciple's feet is as great a joy as to command an army, to follow as to lead, to serve as to rule—when the Holy Guest abides within the soul. Then the soul does not contend for or grasp and hold fast to place and power. It glories rather in fulfilling Paul's exhortation, "Let this mind be in you, which was also in Christ Jesus" (Phil. 2:5 KJV), and it studies Paul's description and illustration of that mind: "Though he was God, he did not think of equality with God as something to cling to. Instead, he gave up his divine privileges; he took the humble position of a slave and was born as a human being. When he appeared in human form, he humbled himself in obedience to God and died a criminal's death on a cross" (Phil. 2:6–8 NLT).

And having thus glimpsed the mind, the character of Christ, the soul yields itself eagerly to the Holy Guest to be conformed to that mind. That is its ambition, its whole desire, its joy and exceeding great reward. To do the will of the Master, to please Him, to win souls for Him, to serve and suffer and sacrifice for and with Him is its great business. But to be like Him, to live in His favor, to fellowship and be in friendship with Him is its life, its great and solemn joy.

When a guest comes into my home—a guest who is high-minded, wise, large of soul, pure of heart, generous in impulse—that person imparts to me something of his or her own nobility. Mean things look meaner, low things sink lower, base things seem baser by comparison, and what is true, honest, just, pure, and lovely (see Phil. 4:8) are the things upon which I would think and about which I would converse. These and these only are the worthwhile things in such a guest's ennobling presence. But if this is so when a mere man or woman, however upright and holy, comes in, how much more when God the Holy Spirit comes in!

Some people lay great stress upon the second coming of Christ as an incentive to fine and holy living, and I would not minimize this. But Jesus said, "When I am raised to life again"—when the Comforter has come in as the Holy Guest—"you will know that I am in my Father, and you are in me, and I am in you" (John 14:20 NLT). In other words, when the Holy Guest abides within, the Father and the Son are there too. And what finer, more searching and sanctifying incentive to holy living can one have than this indwelling presence of Father, Son, and Holy Ghost as Guest of the Soul?

Finally, the great work of this Holy Guest is to exalt Jesus, to glorify Him who humbled Himself unto the shameful and agonizing death of the cross, to make us see Him in all His beauty, to knit our hearts to Him in faith and love and loyalty, to conform us to His image, and to fit us for His work.

The Holy Ghost as Guest within us does not concentrate our attention upon His own person and work, but upon Jesus and His work and sacrifice for us. He does not glorify Himself. He whispers continually of Christ and His example. He points us to Jesus. He would have us "consider the Apostle and High Priest of our profession, Christ Jesus, who was faithful" (Heb. 3:1–2 KJV). He would have us "consider him who endured from sinners such hostility against himself, so that you may not grow weary or fainthearted" (Heb. 12:3 ESV) and feel our cross too heavy to bear. "Even Christ didn't live to please himself" (Rom. 15:3 NLT), He whispered to my friend, who heard the sweet whisper and was content to follow and be as the Master.

When I joined The Salvation Army after having been a Methodist pastor, I was assigned to black the boots of other cadets in the training college. I was tempted to feel it was a dangerous waste of my time, for which my Lord might hold me to account as He did the man who buried his talent instead of investing it. Then the Holy Guest whispered to me of Jesus and pointed me to Him washing the weary and soiled feet of His lowly disciples. And as I saw Jesus, I was content. Any service for Him and His lowly ones, instead of abasing, exalted me.

What we need evermore in every place, at all times, in prosperity and adversity, in health and sickness, in joy and sorrow, in sunshine and shadow, in wealth or grinding poverty, in comfort and distress, in the fellowship and love of friends and in desolation and loneliness, in victory and defeat, in liberty or in prison, in deliverance or temptation, in life and in death—what we need and shall ever need is to see Jesus, and, seeing Him, to walk in His footsteps, "'Who committed no sin, nor was deceit found in His mouth'; who, when He was reviled, did not revile in return; when He suffered, He did not threaten, but committed Himself to Him who judges righteously" (1 Pet. 2:22–23 NKJV).

And this the Holy Guest delights to help us to do as we "watch and pray" (Matt. 26:41 KJV), as we trust and obey. To those who obey Jesus—and only to them—is this Holy Guest given (see Acts 5:32). And when He is given, it is that He may abide as Comforter, Counselor, Helper, and Friend.

NOTE

1. Johann A. Rothe, "Now I Have Found the Ground Wherein," 1727, public domain.

The Trial of Faith Wrought into Experience 4

The world owes an immeasurable debt to Christianity for its treasures of music and song. Jesus sang (see Matt. 26:30). Oh, to have heard Him! And Paul, especially in his letters to the Ephesians and Colossians, exhorts the Christians there to "sing psalms and hymns and spiritual songs to God with thankful hearts," "making music to the Lord in your hearts" (Col. 3:16; Eph. 5:19 NLT). They were to sing to be heard not only by other people, but also by the Lord Himself.

Every great revival of religion results in a revival of singing and of the composition of both music and song. The Franciscan revival in the thirteenth century was marked by exultant singing. And so it was in the days of Luther, the Wesleys, William Booth, and Moody. And so it will always be.

The joys, faith, hopes, and aspirations; the deepest desires; the love and utter devotion; and the sweet trust of the Christian find noblest and freest expression in music and song. And yet it is probable that in no way do people more frequently and yet unconsciously deceive themselves (and actually lie to each other and to God) than in the public singing of songs and hymns.

Languidly, lustily, thoughtlessly in song they profess a faith they do not possess, a love and devotion their whole life falsifies, a joy their lack of radiance on the face and of light in the eye contradicts. They sing, "Oh, how I love Jesus!" while their hearts are far from Him, with no intention of doing the things that please Him. Or while they are restless and defeated, they sing:

> I've wondrous peace through trusting,
>
> A well of joy within;
>
> This rest is everlasting,
>
> My days fresh triumphs bring.[1]

While they live selfishly and spend much of their time in murmuring and complaining instead of praise, they sing:

> Take my life, and let it be
>
> Consecrated, Lord, to Thee;
>
> Take my moments and my days,
>
> Let them flow in ceaseless praise.[2]

It is a solemn thing to stand before God and sing such songs. We should think. A hush should be upon our spirits for we are standing upon holy ground where mysteries are all about us, enshrouding us, while the Angel of the Lord looks upon us through pillar of cloud and fire, and devils leer and lurk to entrap and overthrow us.

Nearly fifty years ago, at The Salvation Army's training school at Clapton, we cadets were singing:

> My will be swallowed up in Thee;
> Light in Thy light still may I see
> In Thine unclouded face.
> Called the full strength of trust to prove.[3]

And there my heart cried out, "Yes, Lord, let me prove the full strength of trust!" And then I was hushed into deep questioning and prayer, for a whisper deep within me asked, "Can you, will you, endure the tests, the trials, that alone can prove the full strength of trust? A feather's weight may test the strength of an infant or an invalid, but heavier and yet heavier weights alone can test the full strength of a man. Will you bear patiently, without murmuring or complaining or fainting, the trials I permit to come upon you, which alone can prove the full strength of your trust and train it for larger service and yet greater trials?"

My humbled heart dared not say, "I can," but only, "By Thy grace I will." And then we continued to sing:

> My will be swallowed up in Thee . . .
> Let all my quickened heart be love,
> My spotless life be praise.[4]

And my whole soul consented to any trial which the Lord in His wisdom and love might permit to come upon me. I willed to be wholly the Lord's, to endure, to "bear up and steer right onward"[5] in the face of every tempest that might blow, every whelming sea that might threaten to engulf me, every huge Goliath who might mock and vow to destroy me. I was not jubilant; my soul was awed into silence, but also into strong confidence and a deep rest of quiet faith.

I felt sure from that hour that if I was to be a saint or soldier of Christ, a winner of souls, and a conqueror on life's battlefields, then I was not to be a pampered pet of the Lord—that I must not expect favors, that my path was not to be strewn with roses, that acclaiming multitudes were not to cheer and crown me, that I must walk by faith, not sight, that I must be faithful and hold fast that which God had given me, that I must still pray when heaven seemed shut and God not listening, that I must rejoice in tribulation and glorify my Lord in the fire, that I must keep hot when others grew cold, stand alone when others ran away, look to no human being for my example but seek always to be an example to all. I knew that I must stand on instant guard against the lure of the world, the insurgence and insistence of the flesh, and the wiles of the Devil, that I must not become sarcastic, cynical, suspicious, or supercilious, but have the love that "thinks no evil . . . bears all things, believes all things, hopes all things, endures all things . . . [and] never fails" (1 Cor. 13:5–8 NKJV), that I must not be seduced by flattery, nor frightened by frowns. I felt that, while esteeming others better than myself (see Phil. 2:3) and in honor preferring others before myself (see Rom. 12:10), and while I was not to be wise in my own conceits (see Rom. 12:16), yet I was in no sense to permit my own personality to be submerged in the mass; that

I must be myself, stand on my own feet, fulfill my own task, bear my own responsibility, answer at last for my own soul, and, when the judgment books are opened, stand or fall by my own record.

That moment when we sang those words was to me most solemn and sacred and not to be forgotten. There God set His seal upon my consenting soul for service, for suffering, for sacrifice. From that moment, life became a thrilling adventure in fellowship with God, in friendship and companionship with Jesus. Everything that has come into my life from that moment has, in some way, by God's sanctifying touch and unfailing grace, enriched me. It may have impoverished me on one side, but it has added to my spiritual wealth on the other, as Jacob's withered thigh, Joseph's slavery and imprisonment, Moses' enforced banishment from Pharaoh's court, and Paul's thorn and shipwrecks and stonings and imprisonments enriched them.

Pain has come to me, but in it I have always found some secret pleasure and compensation. Sorrow and bereavement have thrown me back upon God and deepened and purified my joy in Him. Agony—physical and mental—has led to some unexpected triumphs of grace and faith, and some enlargement of sympathy and power to understand and bless others. Loss and gain, loneliness and love, light and darkness, trials and things hard or impossible to understand—everything has brought its own blessing as my soul has bowed to and accepted the yoke of Jesus and refused to murmur or complain but rather to receive the daily providences of life as God's training school for faith, patience, steadfastness, and love.

Paul was right—and my soul utters a deep "amen"—when he wrote, "And we know that God causes everything to work together for the good

of those who love God and are called according to his purpose for them"
(Rom. 8:28 NLT). Listen to Paul's record of some of the "everything"
which worked together for his good. He had been ridiculed and treated
with scorn by his enemies as an apostle and minister, and he replied:

> Are they servants of Christ? I know I sound like a madman, but
> I have served him far more! I have worked harder, been put in
> prison more often, been whipped times without number, and
> faced death again and again. Five different times the Jewish
> leaders gave me thirty-nine lashes. Three times I was beaten
> with rods. Once I was stoned. Three times I was shipwrecked.
> Once I spent a whole night and a day adrift at sea. I have trav-
> eled on many long journeys. I have faced danger from rivers
> and from robbers. I have faced danger from my own people, the
> Jews, as well as from the Gentiles. I have faced danger in the
> cities, in the deserts, and on the seas. And I have faced danger
> from men who claim to be believers but are not. I have worked
> hard and long, enduring many sleepless nights. I have been hun-
> gry and thirsty and have often gone without food. I have shivered
> in the cold, without enough clothing to keep me warm.
>
> Then, besides all this, I have the daily burden of my concern
> for all the churches. (2 Cor. 11:23–28 NLT)

What a list, and it is not complete! A study of his Corinthian letters
reveals much more of his mental and spiritual trials and conflicts
which meant unmeasured suffering to his sensitive soul, so chaste in
its purity, so keenly alive to all the finest and loftiest views of life,

and so hungry for human as well as divine love and fellowship. This was a man who gloried in his tribulations, because they worked in him patience, experience, and hope (see Rom. 5:3–4), and he declared that in all things he was more than conqueror (see Rom. 8:37). Indeed, he called those things a "light affliction, which is but for a moment" (2 Cor. 4:17 KJV).

He looked at them in the light of eternity, and they were so swallowed up in that vastness, that infinitude, that he said they were "but for a moment." And then he added that such afflictions are actually "working for us"—our slave, working out for us—"a far more exceeding and eternal weight of glory, while we do not look at the things which are seen, but at the things which are not seen. For the things which are seen are temporary [fleeting, soon to pass away and be forgotten], but the things which are not seen are eternal" (2 Cor. 4:17–18 NKJV).

Paul said, "We know"—his uncertainties, doubts, fears, questionings, had all vanished, being swallowed up in knowledge—"that God causes everything to work together for the good of those who love God" (Rom. 8:28 NLT).

But how did he know? How had Paul reached such happy assurance? He knew by faith. He believed God, and light on dark problems streamed into his soul through faith.

He knew by joyful union with the risen Christ, who had conquered death and the grave. This union was so real that Christ's victory was his victory also.

He knew in part by experience. Paul had suffered much, and by experience he had found all things in the past working for his good, enriching his spiritual life through the abounding grace of his Lord.

And this gave him assurance for "everything" and for all the future. Nothing could really harm him while he was in the divine will, in the eternal order, while he was a branch in the living Vine, a member of Christ's body (see Rom. 12:5; 1 Cor. 12:20–27).

Listen to him: "Can anything ever separate us from Christ's love? Does it mean he no longer loves us if we have trouble or calamity, or are persecuted, or hungry, or destitute, or in danger, or threatened with death? . . . No, despite all these things, overwhelming victory is ours through Christ, who loved us" (Rom. 8:35, 37 NLT).

Hear Paul again: "We can rejoice, too, when we run into problems and trials, for we know that they help us develop endurance. And endurance develops strength of character, and character strengthens our confident hope of salvation. And this hope will not lead to disappointment. For we know how dearly God loves us, because he has given us the Holy Spirit to fill our hearts with his love" (Rom. 5:3–5 NLT).

Hear him yet once more: "And I am convinced that nothing can ever separate us from God's love. Neither death nor life, neither angels nor demons, neither our fears for today nor our worries about tomorrow — not even the powers of hell can separate us from God's love. No power in the sky above or in the earth below — indeed, nothing in all creation will ever be able to separate us from the love of God that is revealed in Christ Jesus our Lord" (Rom. 8:38–39 NLT).

Any and everything, present and future, which produced patience, experience of God's love, and hope in Him, Paul was sure was working for his good, and he welcomed it with rejoicing, for it came bearing gifts of spiritual riches. That is how he knew. We may believe what is revealed in the Bible about this and enter into peace, great peace, but we come to know, as Paul did, by putting God and life to the test—by experience.

I happened to be present when a young wife and mother was weeping bitter tears of anguish. An older wife and mother, with a face like the morning, full of heaven's own peace, who had herself wept bitter tears of anguish, put her arms around the younger woman and in tender and wise words of perfect assurance comforted her. And as I noted the gentleness, wisdom, calmness, and moral strength of the elder woman, I thought, "Ah, her trials that were so painful worked for her good. They left her enlarged in heart, enriched in experience and knowledge, sweetened in character, wise in sympathy, calm in storm, perfect in peace, and with a spirit at home and at rest in God while yet in the body."

And I looked forward with joy in the hope that the younger woman, believing in Jesus, patiently submitting to chastening and trials as opportunities for the exercise and the discipline of faith, would enter into an experience of God's love and faithfulness that would leave her spirit forever strengthened, sweetened, enriched, and fitted to comfort and strengthen others. And so, after years, it proved to be.

Our true good in this and all worlds is spiritual. And trials, afflictions, losses, and sorrows, borne with patience and courage and in faith, will surely develop in us spiritual graces and "the peaceful fruit of righteousness" (Heb. 12:11 ESV) which are never found in those whose sky is never overcast, whose voyage over life's sea is never troubled by storm and hurricane, whose soldiering is only on dress parade and never in deadly battle, or who, facing storm or battle, flee away and so escape it.

Holiness of heart does not ensure us against painful things that try our faith, but it does prepare us for the trial, while the patient endurance of trial reveals the reality of our faith, the purity and integrity of our hearts, and the grace and faithfulness of our Lord.

When Abraham was tried in the offering up of Isaac, the angel of the Lord said, "Now I know that you truly fear God. You have not withheld from me even your son, your only son" (Gen. 22:12 NLT). And again and again the most obstinate opponents of Christianity have been conquered by the patient endurance and the radiant joy of suffering Christians. It was so not only in the days of far-off persecutions—in Rome, when Christians were thrown to the wild beasts, roasted over slow fires, tortured in every conceivable way—but also in our own day and in the history of The Salvation Army that the blood of the martyrs and the patience and triumphant joy of the saints have won the hardest skeptics to Jesus.

Paul looked upon his sufferings as a part of the sufferings of Christ, as though Christ's sufferings did not end upon the cross but were completed in the sufferings of His disciples. Paul wrote, "I am glad when I suffer for you in my body, for I am participating in the sufferings of Christ that continue for his body, the church" (Col. 1:24 NLT).

Happy are we if we can receive all suffering in that spirit, whether it is suffering of body, mind, or soul. It will then work for our good and through us for the good of others, whether or not we can understand how it is to do so.

It will purge us of vanity. It will deepen us in humility, enlarge us in sympathy, and make us more fruitful in the graces of the Spirit.

How bitter that cup
No tongue can conceive,
Which He drank quite up

That sinners might live.

His way was much rougher

And darker than mine:

Did Christ, my Lord, suffer,

And shall I repine?

Since all that I meet

Shall work for my good,

The bitter is sweet,

The medicine is food;

Though painful at present,

'Twill cease before long,

And then, oh, how pleasant

The conqueror's song![6]

NOTES

1. John Lawley, "Come, with Me Visit Calvary," 1905, public domain.

2. Frances Ridley Havergal, "Take My Life and Let It Be," 1874, public domain.

3. Charles Wesley, "Come, Holy Ghost, All-Quickening Fire," 1739, public domain.

4. Ibid.

5. John Milton, "To the Same," 1655, public domain.

6. John Newton, "Begone, Unbelief! My Savior Is Near," 1779, public domain.

A Perfect-Hearted People 5

God is looking for people whose hearts are perfect toward Him—a perfected-hearted people; so there is a kind of perfection required of His people by God.

A friend asked me some time ago whether I believed in and taught perfection. I replied that that depended upon what he meant by the term *perfection*.

If he meant absolute perfection, I did not. Nor did I believe in the possession by humans of angelic perfection, nor yet in their realizing such perfection as Adam must have originally possessed.

God alone is absolutely perfect in all His attributes, and to such perfection we can never hope to attain. There is also a perfection possessed by the angels, which we shall never have in this world. Adam also had certain perfections of body and mind which are out of our reach.

There is, however, a perfection which we are given to understand God requires in us. It is a perfection not of head but of heart—not of knowledge but of goodness, humility, love, and faith. Such a perfection God desires us to have, and such a perfection we may have.

In saying this, I cannot be accused of being a crank or a fanatic, for I am proclaiming only the plain, simple truth as it is revealed in God's Word, and we ought to desire to rise up to all the privileges God has conferred upon us.

"Be perfect, even as your Father in heaven is perfect," said Jesus (Matt. 5:48 NLT). What sort of perfection is this that we are to possess? God is a Spirit; we are simply men and women. And further, "No one has ever seen God" (John 1:18 NLT). How then are we to know what that perfection is which He requires of us—a perfection which it is possible for men and women to manifest? In this, Jesus is our pattern. It is true that "no one has ever seen God. But the unique One, who is himself God, is near to the Father's heart. He has revealed God to us" (John 1:18 NLT). That is, Jesus manifested the Father's nature and perfections in a human life that we can see and understand.

This perfection of heart, of purity, and of goodness, was seen in Jesus in several particulars, and in these we are to follow His example.

We are to be perfectly submitted to God. We are to come to the place where we no longer fight against God's will, where we do not complain or talk back or resist, but yield in perfect submission to all His will.

In the terrible burning of the ferry *The General Slocum* in New York Harbor in 1904, almost all the mothers and children of one church lost their lives. The next Sunday the bereaved fathers and husbands came to the church, and the pastor—who had lost his whole family—rose and said, "The LORD gave, and the LORD has taken away; blessed be the name of the LORD" (Job 1:21 ESV). Those men were perfectly submissive to God in their hearts, and they did not fight against God's providences nor fail God in the hour of their suffering and trial.

It is possible to be submitted to God in this way. We may not understand God's providences, but we can say "amen" to them from our hearts.

Like Jesus, we may perfectly trust God. We may possess a confidence in God that holds out in ways we do not understand, like the confidence a very little child has in a parent, that will trust mother or father with all the heart.

Job was rich, prosperous, and happy. Then trouble came. He was afflicted. He lost his children. He lost his property, and his herds were carried off by marauders. What did Job do? He did not complain and blame God, but said, "The LORD gave, and the LORD has taken away; blessed be the name of the LORD" (Job 1:21 ESV). And when his faithless wife advised him to curse God and die, Job defended God's way and said, "'You speak as one of the foolish women would speak. Shall we receive good from God, and shall we not receive evil?' In all this Job did not sin with his lips" (Job 2:10 ESV).

Then his friends tried to shake his confidence, and Job—afflicted, full of pain, poor, and bereaved of his children—seemed to be forsaken by God. But he looked up from his ash heap and exclaimed, "Though he slay me, yet will I trust in him" (Job 13:15 KJV).

It is always so with the perfect-hearted man or woman. I want my friends to trust me, and if they failed to do so when I was out of their sight it would break my heart. So God wants us to trust Him where we cannot see Him.

Paul and Silas, on one of their missionary journeys, were arrested and placed in one of those loathsome Roman prisons—in the inmost, wet, slimy, foul dungeon—with the wounds on their backs from the scourging they had just received gaping wide and with their feet in the stocks. But they did not worry and complain and determine to go home when they were released. They sang and praised the Lord.

That is the kind of spirit God wants His people to possess: a spirit that will rejoice with a perfect trust in Him under adversity.

God desires His people to be perfect in love, to love Him perfectly. We are not expected to love God with the heart of an archangel, for we are only poor humble souls with limited power to love, but God does expect us to love with all our hearts—with all our power to love.

The little child is to love with all his or her power. And as our powers develop and grow, our love is to develop and grow apace with our power to love. But we are always to love with all the heart.

There must be perfect loyalty. Love is not an emotion, a happy feeling. It is not something on the surface. It is a deep principle, revealing itself in perfect loyalty to God.

What constitutes a perfect husband or wife, or son or daughter? Imagine a big, ignorant young man who could not shine in a social situation. He is hardworking, rough, uncultured, and awkward, and in the eyes of the world is a most imperfect man. But he has a dear old mother whom he loves. He works to give her his meager wages at the end of the week. He carries up the coal to heat her rooms. And when his day's work is done he comes home to cheer his old mother with his presence. He does all he can to make her latter days comfortable and happy. He is a very imperfect man, but his mother would tell you with pride, "He is my perfect son." What makes him a perfect son? Perfect loyalty to his old mother.

So our heart may be perfect if it beats in perfect loyalty to God—wholly yielded up to fulfill all His purposes. We may be very imperfect as a man or woman, and our imperfections may be apparent to everyone. We may blunder and make many mistakes. We may be ignorant and uncultured. Yet God looks down and counts us a perfect-hearted person. When God sees a heart perfect in loyalty to Him, He overlooks many mistakes and blunders of the head.

God also requires of us perfect obedience. Our performance may not always be perfect, but our spirit may be perfect.

God's eyes are in all parts of the earth, seeking for men and women with hearts perfect toward Him in submission, trust, love, and obedience. And when He finds such a heart, He reveals Himself to that person and shows Himself on behalf of him or her.

Now let me ask you, what kind of heart do you have? Have you submitted to Him? Have you consecrated yourself wholly to Him? Have you put all your powers at His disposal? Have you let Him have all His way with you? How anger and pride and selfishness and uncleanness must grieve Him! The perfect-hearted person has put all these things away.

How can I put away these things that seem to be a part of my very being? How can I change the color of my eyes or add a cubit to my stature? I cannot! Work as I will, I shall always fail to change my moral nature. But God can. It is His work.

If we go down before Him in complete humility and say, "Lord, I am willing to have my heart changed. Though it may mean that I shall be despised and hated and persecuted, I will take up my cross; I will crucify myself. I am willing that my selfishness and pride and hate and uncleanness shall be taken from me, and that You shall reign in me and create in me a clean heart, perfect in its love, submission, loyalty, trust, and obedience"—if we will say that to Him, He will answer our prayer today, now, this moment, if we will but believe.

A Thirteenth-Century Salvationist 6

Most of the Ten Commandments can be made into laws of the land by legislative enactment, but not so the Sermon on the Mount. It is not only a sin to murder and steal; it is also a crime, a breach of law. But no statesman has ever yet passed a law compelling people to be poor in spirit, meek, merciful, pure of heart, loving to enemies, and glad when lied about and persecuted. Human beings may be restrained by the strong hand of the law from stealing or committing murder, but they can be constrained to be meek and lowly in heart, to bless them who curse them, to pray for them who despitefully use them, and to love those who hate them only by grace.

"The law was given by Moses, but grace and truth came by Jesus Christ" (John 1:17 KJV). He was "full of grace and truth" (John 1:14 KJV). When His heart broke on Calvary it was like the breaking of Mary's alabaster box of ointment. And when He poured out the Holy Spirit at

Pentecost, rivers of grace and truth began to stream forth to every land, to all people.

The nature religions and philosophies of the Gentile world and the religion of the scribes and Pharisees, sunk into legal forms and ceremonies, were powerless to give peace to troubled consciences, strength to slaves of vice and corruption, or life to souls that were dead in sin. But that is just what the grace of God in Christ did. It met and fitted men and women's moral and spiritual needs as light meets the eye, as the skin fits the hand.

What happened when Paul went to luxurious, licentious Corinth and preached Christ to the reveling populace? Fornicators, idolaters, adulterers, homosexuals, thieves, covetous people, drunkards, and revelers became saints. Their eyes were opened, their darkness vanished, their chains fell off, and they received "beauty for ashes, the oil of joy for mourning, the garment of praise for the spirit of heaviness" (Isa. 61:3 KJV). Christ made them free. They loved each other. They lived in close association with each other, but they did not shut themselves away from their non-Christian neighbors. They went everywhere declaring the good news of redeeming love and uttermost salvation in Christ.

But not all who named the name of Christ departed from iniquity. Heresies crept in. Persecutions arose. The awful corruptions and subtle philosophies of the heathen world undermined the morals, weakened the courage, and dimmed or destroyed the faith of many. The whole social and political order of the ancient world began to crumble. The Roman Empire fell before the assaults of northern barbarians, and the Dark Ages supervened. The secret of salvation and sanctification by faith, which made Paul's converts in Corinth victorious over the proud and putrid world in which they lived, the flesh which had enslaved them, and the Devil who had deceived them, was largely, if not wholly, lost.

Earnest souls, sick of sin, weary of strife, and ignorant of the way of victorious faith in an indwelling Christ, fled to the desert and wilderness to escape temptation. Many of them became hermits, living solitary lives on pillars in the desert and in dens and caves of the earth, while others formed monastic communities of monks and nuns. They harked back to the grim austerity and asceticism of Elijah and John the Baptist, and lost the sweet reasonableness and holy naturalness of Jesus. In the solitude of desert dens and the darkness of wilderness caves and on the tops of lonely pillars they kept painful vigil and fought bitter battles with devils. With prolonged fastings and flagellations they struggled to overcome the unsanctified passions of the flesh.

There were saints among these seekers, who found God and kept sacred learning and faith alive. It was the hermit St. Jerome who translated the Scriptures into the common language, giving us the version known as the Vulgate. It was the monk Thomas à Kempis who wrote *The Imitation of Christ*. Some of the sweetest and most stirring hymns of Christendom leaped forth from glad and loving hearts in monasteries of the Dark Ages. Those ages were dark, but not wholly dark.

As the iron empire of Rome, corroded and rusted by luxury and utterly corrupt vices, began to crumble and fall before the fierce, barbaric hordes of the north, feudalism sprang up and the great mass of people became serfs who tilled the fields and fought the wars of petty lords who lived in castles overlooking the towns and villages that dotted the plains. Towns and cities, torn and reddened by internal factional strife, made war on each other. The baron made war on his enemy, the rich abbot, and endowed and adorned his castle and church with spoils of his petty warfare. The clergy were generally greedy and corrupt. Poverty, illiteracy, filth, and disease were universal. Brigands infested the forests and mountains, and pitiful, loathsome lepers begged for alms along the highways.

At the end of a thousand years of such dimness and darkness, when a new dawn was breaking (which he was greatly to hasten), St. Francis of Assisi appeared. He was the son of a prosperous Italian cloth merchant and a gentle and devout French lady who probably sprang from the nobility. A beautiful, courteous lad, with flashing eyes and equally flashing spirit, who sang the songs of the troubadours in his mother's native tongue and delighted in the sports and revelry and daredevil doings of the youth of the town—such was Francis Bernadone. Little did he seem to have in him the stuff of a saint who would transform the Christendom of his day and hold the wondering and affectionate gaze of seven centuries. His father was a tradesman, but he was rich and freehanded with his dashing and attractive son.

The boy was lavish with money and courteous and lively in spirit, which made him the friend and companion of the young nobility who dwelt in castles. War broke out between Assisi and the city of Perugia, so Francis, burning with the pride of youth and the fires of patriotism, went forth with the young noblemen and their bands of serfs to fight the enemy. But the battle went against the Assisians, and a company of the leaders—including Francis—were captured and spent a year in prison.

The youthful aristocrats, deprived of liberty, languished. But Francis, whom they kept among them, never lost his spirit, but cheered his companions with his kindness, his gaiety, and his songs. He laughed and sang and made merry, and possibly partly in jest but more in earnest, through some strange youthful premonition, he assured them that he would one day be a great prince, with his name on the lips of all. Little did he or they suspect what kind of a prince he would be, or the nature of the acclaim with which people would greet him.

Months of sickness followed his imprisonment. He began to think on the things that are eternal, the things of the spirit. Recovered from his illness, he went forth again on a fine steed, in glittering armor, to war. But, for some rather obscure reason, he returned and fell into strange meditative moods. His companions suspected that it was an affair of the heart and asked him if he was dreaming of a lady love. He admitted that he was—a fairer love than they had ever imagined: Lady Poverty! He was thinking of giving up all for Christ.

One day while Francis was serving a customer in his father's shop, a beggar came in and asked for alms in the name of God. Francis, busy with his customer, sent him away empty-handed, but afterward said to himself, "If he had asked in the name of some nobleman, how promptly and generously I should have responded. But he asked in the name of the Lord, and I sent him away with nothing!" Leaving the shop, he ran after the beggar and lavished money upon him, and from that day he was the unfailing friend of beggars and all the poor.

Lepers were peculiarly repulsive to him, and he stood in a kind of fear of them. One day when riding, he met a leper, and a fear he would not have felt on a field of battle gripped him. He rode past the poor creature and then, ashamed of himself, won a greater victory than ever was won by armed warriors on a field of blood. He wheeled his horse around and returned, and leaping down, he kissed the leper and gave him all the money he had with him. Joy filled his heart, and ever after he was the friend, the benefactor, and the frequent nurse and companion of lepers.

He was a creature of generous, self-sacrificing impulse. But once he yielded to the impulse it became a lifelong principle, and he served it with the unfailing devotion of a lover to his mistress. However, like little Samuel, he "did not yet know the Lord, neither was the word of the Lord yet revealed unto him" (1 Sam. 3:7 KJV). But one day he was praying before the altar in a poor, half-ruined little church: "Great and glorious God, and Thou, Lord Jesus, I pray, shed abroad Thy light in the darkness of my mind. Be found of me, O Lord, so in all things I may act only in accordance with Thy holy will." His eyes were upon a crucifix as he prayed, and it seemed to him that the Savior's eyes met his. The place suddenly became a holy place, and he was in the presence of the Lord and Savior as was Moses when he drew near the burning bush on Horeb.

The sacred Victim seemed alive, and as a Voice spoke to Moses from the bush, so a wondrous, sweet, ineffable Voice seemed to speak from the crucifix to the longing soul of Francis, bidding him to repair the church that was falling into decay and ruin. From that day he was assured that Christ knew him, heard him, loved him, and wanted his service. He could say, "I am my beloved's, and my beloved is mine" (Song 6:3 KJV).

Francis was essentially a man of action rather than of contemplation, so instead of retiring to a hermit's lodge in the desert or a monastery on some hilltop, he sallied forth at once to repair the little church of St. Damien in which he had been praying and had heard the Voice. He begged stones and carried them himself, repairing the church with his own hands. And when that was completed he repaired yet another church. It had not yet dawned upon him that the Voice was calling him to repair, not the four walls of a church made with hands, but the spiritual church with its living stones not built with hands.

His proud and disappointed father fell upon him, beat him, and imprisoned him in his home. But during the absence of his father, his mother released him and he returned to the church, where he lived with the priest, wearing—instead of his rich clothing—a hair shirt and a rough brown robe tied around him with a rope, which was later to become the uniform of the myriad brothers of the Franciscan order. He worked or begged for his bread and in Assisi was looked upon as a madman. His father and brother cursed him when they saw him.

He publicly renounced all right to his patrimony and adopted utter poverty as one of the rules of his life. He made poverty one of the rules—indeed, the most distinctive rule of the order he founded. And later, when the bishop of Assisi gently reproved him and argued that he should not go to such an extreme, he silenced the bishop, who had trouble with his own riches, by shrewdly replying, "If we own property we must have laws and arms to defend them, and this will destroy love out of our hearts."

In a short time—as with a true Salvationist, or any true Christian— the sincerity, sweetness, joy, and devotion of his life began to disarm criticism, win approval, and cause heart searchings in many of his fellow townspeople.

His first convert was a wealthy man called Bernardo, who had been impressed by Francis's joyous, simple life. He invited Francis to spend the night with him and only simulated sleep that he might watch the young man. When Francis thought he was asleep, he knelt by his bedside and spent most of the night in prayer. The next morning Bernardo, who became one of the most noted and devout of the brothers, decided to sell all, give to the poor, and cast in his lot with Francis.

A third, named Pietro, joined them, and the three went to church where, after praying and examining the Scriptures, they adopted as the rule of their new life the words of Jesus: "If you want to be perfect, go and sell all your possessions and give the money to the poor, and you will have treasure in heaven. Then come, follow me" (Matt. 19:21 NLT).

Jesus called together his twelve disciples and gave them power and authority to cast out all demons and to heal all diseases. Then he sent them out to tell everyone about the Kingdom of God and to heal the sick. "Take nothing for your journey," he instructed them. "Don't take a walking stick, a traveler's bag, food, money, or even a change of clothes. Wherever you go, stay in the same house until you leave town. And if a town refuses to welcome you, shake its dust from your feet as you leave to show that you have abandoned those people to their fate."

So they began their circuit of the villages, preaching the Good News and healing the sick. (Luke 9:1–6 NLT)

The literal strictness with which Francis and his early disciples followed and enforced the rule of utter poverty gave them great freedom from care, great freedom of movement, and much joy. But later, this led to much strife and division in the order, the beginnings of which in his lifetime saddened the last days of the saint.

The pope sanctioned Francis's rule and granted him and the members of the order the right to preach. Like the early disciples, they went everywhere testifying, singing, preaching, laboring with their hands for food, and, when unable to get work, not hesitating to ask from door to door for bread.

At first they were scorned and often beaten, but they gloried in tribulation. "My brothers, commit yourselves to God with all your cares and He will care for you," said Francis, and they went with joy, strictly observing his instructions:

Let us consider that God in His goodness has called us not merely for our own salvation, but also for that of many men, that we may go through all the world exhorting men, more by our example than by our words, to repent of their sins and keep the commandments. Be not fearful because we appear little and ignorant. Have faith in God, that His Spirit will speak in and by you.

You will find men, full of faith, gentleness, and goodness, who will receive you and your words with joy; but you will find others, and in great numbers, faithless, proud, blasphemers, who will speak evil of you, resisting you and your words. Be resolute, then, to endure everything with patience and humility.

Have no fear, for very soon many noble and learned men will come to you; they will be with you preaching to kings and princes and to a multitude of people. Many will be converted to the Lord all over the world, who will multiply and increase His family.[1]

How like William Booth, the founder of The Salvation Army, that sounds!

And what he preached, Francis practiced to the end. He died prematurely, surrounded by his first followers, exhausted, blind, and, at his own request, stripped except for a hair shirt and laid upon the bare ground. His rule, his order, and his life and example were a stern and mighty rebuke to the wealth, greed, and laziness of the priests and the monks. But he exhorted his brothers not to judge others, not to condemn or be severe, but to honor them, give them all due respect and pray for them, remembering some whom they might think to be members of the Devil would yet become members of Christ.

Within a brief time, five thousand friars in brown robes were going everywhere with their glad songs, their burning exhortations, their simple testimony and sacrificial lives, and all who met them met with a spiritual adventure not to be forgotten. In Spain, some of them fell upon martyrdom. They went to Germany, France, and to far Scandinavia, where they built the great cathedral of Upsala. Francis himself went to the Holy Land with the crusaders, and at the risk of his life, boldly entered the camp of the Saracens with two of his brothers and sought to convert the Saracen leader and his host. In this he failed, but he made a deep impression on the followers of Mohammed.

Once he was called to preach before the pope and the College of Cardinals. He carefully prepared his sermon, but when he attempted to deliver it he became confused, frankly confessed his confusion, forgot his prepared address, threw himself upon the Lord, and spoke from his heart as moved by the Spirit—spoke with such love and fire that he burned into all hearts and melted his august audience to many tears. Long before Hus and Luther appeared, thundering against the abuses of the church, Francis wrought a great reformation by love, simplicity, and self-sacrifice. He was a kindred spirit of George Fox and John Wesley and William Booth, and would have gloried in their fellowship.

After seven centuries, his words are still as sweet as honey, as searching as fire, as penetrating and revealing as light. One winter's day, bitterly cold, he was journeying with a Brother Leo, when he said:

May it please God that the Brothers Minor [the "Little Brothers," the name he adopted for the Franciscan order] all over the world may give a great example of holiness and edification. But not in this is the perfect joy. If the Little Brothers gave sight to the blind, healed the sick, cast out demons, gave hearing to the deaf, or even raised the four-days' dead—not in this is the perfect joy.

If a Brother Minor knew all languages, all science, and all Scripture, if he could prophesy and reveal not only future things, but even the secret of consciences and of souls—not in this consists the perfect joy.

If he could speak the language of angels; if he knew the courses of the stars and the virtues of plants; if all the treasures of earth were revealed to him, and he knew the qualities of birds, fishes, and all animals, of men, trees, rocks, roots, and waters—not in these is the perfect joy.

"Father, in God's name, I pray you," exclaimed Leo, "Tell me in what consists the perfect joy."

"When we arrive at Santa Maria degli Angeli, soaked with rain, frozen with cold, covered with mud, dying of hunger," said Francis, "and we knock, and the porter comes in a rage, saying 'Who are you?' and we answer, 'We are two of your brethren,' and he says, 'You lie; you are two lewd fellows who go up and down corrupting the world and stealing the alms of the poor. Go away!' and he does not open to us, but leaves us outside in the snow and rain, frozen, starved, all night—then, if thus maltreated and turned away we patiently endure all without murmuring against him; if we think with humility and charity that this porter really knows us truly and that God makes him speak thus to us, in this is the perfect joy. Above all the graces and all the gifts which the Holy Spirit gives to His friends is the grace to conquer one's self, and willingly to suffer pain, outrages, disgrace, and evil treatment for the love of Christ."[2]

This sounds like echoes from the Sermon on the Mount and the epistles and testimonies of Paul. It is a commentary upon Paul's psalm of love in the thirteenth chapter of 1 Corinthians, and on his testimony: "I take pleasure in infirmities, in reproaches, in necessities, in persecutions, in distresses for Christ's sake" (2 Cor. 12:10 KJV).

It is a commentary on the words of Jesus—"Life is not measured by how much you own" (Luke 12:15 NLT)—and on those other, often forgotten and neglected words: "Blessed are you when others revile you and persecute you and utter all kinds of evil against you falsely on my account. Rejoice and be glad, for your reward is great in heaven, for so they persecuted the prophets who were before you" (Matt. 5:11–12 ESV).

Francis had found the secret of joy, power, purity, and of that enduring influence which still stirs and draws out the hearts of people of faith, simplicity, and steadfastness. Across the centuries, he speaks to us in a wooing, compelling message that humbles us at the feet of Jesus in contrition and adoring wonder and love.

He found hidden reservoirs of power in union with Christ; in following Christ; in counting all things loss for Christ; in meekly sharing the labors, the travail, the passion, and the cross of Christ. Thus his life became creative instead of acquisitive. He became a builder, a fighter, a creator. He found his joy, his fadeless glory, his undying influence, not in possessing things, not in attaining rank and title and worldly pomp and power, but in building the spiritual house, the kingdom of God—in fighting the battles of the Lord against the hosts of sin and hate and selfishness.

This creative life he found in the way of sacrifice and service. He found his life by losing it. He laid down his life and found it again, found it multiplied a thousand fold, found it being reproduced in myriads of others.

And this I conceive to be the supreme lesson of the life of Francis for us today. For it remains eternally true, it is a law of the Spirit, it is the everlasting word of Jesus, that "whoever finds his life will lose it, and whoever loses his life for my sake will find it" (Matt. 10:39 ESV).

O Lord, help me; help Your people everywhere; help the greedy, grasping, stricken world to learn what these words of the Master mean and to put them to the test with the deathless, sacrificial ardor of the simple, selfless saint of Assisi!

I knew that Christ had given me birth
To brother all the souls of earth,
And every bird and every beast
Should share the crumbs broke at the feast.[3]

NOTES

1. Source unknown.

2. Possibly drawn from an account in *Life of St. Francis of Assisi* by Paul Sabatier (New York: Charles Scribner's Sons, 1917), 138–139.

3. John Masefield, "The Everlasting Mercy," 1917, public domain.

Looking Backward and Forward 7

Seventy years are less than a pinpoint in the vastness of God's eternity, but they are a long, long time in the life of a man. When I was a child, a man of seventy seemed to me to be as old as the hills. I stood in awe of him. No words could express how venerable he was. When I looked up to him it was like looking up to the snowy, sun-crowned, storm-swept heights of great mountains.

And now, having lived threescore years and ten,[1] I feel as one who has scaled a mighty mountain, done an exploit, or won a war. What toil it has involved! What dangers have been met and overcome! What dull routine, what thrilling adventure! What love, what joy and sorrow, what defeats and victories, what hopes and fears! What visions and dreams yet to be fulfilled! And the river not far away, yet to be crossed. "My soul, be on thy guard!"[2] I remember and marvel.

Yet I feel I am but a child. At times I feel as frisky as a boy and I have stoutly to repress myself to keep from behaving frivolously. And I hear my friend, brother, mentor, and companion of half a century, Paul, saying, "Older men are to be sober-minded, dignified, self-controlled" (Titus 2:2 ESV). Then again I feel as old as I am. The leaden weight of seventy years presses heavily upon me.

I look back and it seems like centuries since I was a carefree little lad. Then some vivid memory will leap up within me, and the seventy years seem like a tale of yesterday and I am again a "wee little boy with the tousled head"[3] playing around the flower-embowered cottage in the tiny village by the little Blue River where I was born.

The average age of man is much less than seventy years, so I am a leftover from a departed generation. But while the snows of seventy winters are on my head, the sunshine of seventy summers is in my heart. The fading, falling leaves of seventy autumns solemnize my soul, but the resurrection life up-springing in flower and tree; the returning songbirds; the laughing, leaping brooks and swelling rivers; and the sweet, soft winds of seventy springtimes gladden me.

A history of the world during these seventy years would show such an advance socially, politically, educationally, economically, scientifically, and morally as has not been seen during any previous thousand years of recorded history. People without a background of knowledge of history may dispute this, but as desperate as the moral, social, and economic conditions of great masses are today, those who know the story of the ages will not dispute it.

Women no longer have to be mistresses and playthings of prime ministers and kings to influence the political destinies of nations. They now sit as men's equal in parliament and senate, proclaim from pulpit and platform the gospel of God's holiness and redeeming love, and are mistress of their own fortune and person.

Childhood is protected by law. Human trafficking, while still carried on, is outlawed by civilized nations. Human slavery and serfdom have been swept away among all but the least advanced peoples. Africa has been opened to the light of civilization and the gospel, and its open sores are being healed. The cannibal islands have been evangelized, and shipwrecked sailors and missionaries are safe on their shore.

When I was a child, it took weeks to communicate with Europe and months to reach Asia. Today, King George speaks words of welcome in London to the peace envoys of nations, and the whole world listens in. We in America hear his royal voice five hours before he spoke, according to our clocks! Admiral Byrd at the South Pole speaks, and we hear him over twelve thousand miles of land and sea before his voice could reach his companion one hundred feet away! Time and space are conquered, and the whole world has become one vast whispering gallery since I was a child.

Diseases which had scourged humankind from time immemorial are now being banished from the earth. War, as the policy of nations, is renounced and denounced. Open diplomacy is an accomplished fact.

Wealth is now looked upon as a trust for humanity. Instead of fitting out pirate ships and ravaging the coasts of China as would have been done long ago, Mr. Rockefeller gives millions to establish one of the most beautiful and up-to-date hospitals and medical schools in the world in Beijing, and untold millions are cabled across the ocean to feed the starving peoples.

When I consider the vanishing darkness, the toppling thrones, the crumbling empires, the fallen crowns, the outlawed tyrannies, the mastery of nature's secrets, the harnessing of the earth's exhaustless energies, the penetration of all lands with the story and light of the gospel, which I have witnessed in my day, I can't help but feel that I was born at the beginning of the end of the Dark Ages.

But while the light increases and widens, the darkness still does not comprehend it. And while God's "truth is marching on,"[4] "evil people and impostors . . . flourish" (2 Tim. 3:13 NLT), become more and more self-conscious and class-conscious, and organize and mass themselves to fight against God and His Christ and His saints and soldiers more subtly and determinedly than at any time since the days of the Roman persecutions and the Spanish Inquisition—and this may result in:

> Vast eddies in the flood
> Of onward time . . .
> And throned races may degrade.[5]

This makes me wish for the strength of youth that I might share in the battles yet to be. But that is denied me. I must go on, like Tennyson's ships, "to the haven under the hill."[6] But I go on serene in unshaken confidence that the flood, in spite of all eddies, flows onward not backward, that the light will evermore increase, and that any triumph of "evil people and impostors" will be short.

Many of God's children are longing for Jesus to come in person, visibly to lead His hosts to victory. But ever since that wonderful morning forty-five years ago when He baptized me with the Holy Spirit and fire, purifying my heart and revealing Himself within me, I have felt that He meant to win His triumphs through dead men and women—dead to sin, to the world, to its prizes and praises, and all alive to Him, filled with His Spirit, indwelt by His presence, burning with His love, glad with His joy, enduring with His patience, thrilled with His hope, daring with His self-renunciation and courage, being consumed with His zeal, all-conquering with His faith, rejoicing in "the fellowship of his sufferings," and gladly made "conformable unto his death" (Phil. 3:10 KJV). I expect the true Vine to show forth all its strength, its beauty, and its fruitfulness through the branches.

I do not expect the love of the Father; the eternal intercession of the risen and enthroned Son; the wise and loving and ceaseless ministry of conviction, conversion, regeneration, and sanctification of the Holy Spirit; and the prayers, preaching, sacrifice, and holy living of the soldiers of Jesus and saints of God to fail. Jesus is even now leading on His hosts to victory.

I cannot always—if ever—comprehend His great strategy. My small sector of the vast battlefield may be covered with smoke and thick darkness. The mocking foe may be pressing hard, friends may fear and falter and flee, and the Enemy may apparently triumph as he did when Jesus died and when the martyrs perished in sheets of flame, by the sword and headman's axe, mauled by the lion's paw, crunched by the tiger's tooth, and slain by the serpent's fang. But the Enemy's triumph always has been and always will be short, for Jesus is leading on and up, ever on, ever up, never backward, never downward, always forward, ever toward the rising sun. Revivals, resurrection life and power, are resident in our religion. A dead church may, when we least expect, flame with revival fire, for Jesus, though unseen, is on the battlefield, and He is leading on. "I am with you always, even to the end of the age" (Matt. 28:20 NLT).

In the lonely and still night, while others sleep, He stirs some longing soul to sighs and tears and strong crying and wrestling prayer. He kindles utter, deathless devotion in that soul, a consuming jealousy for God's glory, for the salvation of others, for the coming of the kingdom of God. And in that lonely and still night and out of that travail, that agony of spirit mingled with solemn joy, a revival is born. "The Kingdom of God can't be detected by visible signs" (Luke 17:20 NLT). There may be no blast of trumpets, no thunder of drums, no flaunting of flags. The revival is born in the heart of some lonely, longing, wrestling, believing, importunate man or woman who will give God no rest, who will not let Him go until He blesses. Bright-eyed, golden-haired, rosy-cheeked dolls can be made by machinery and turned out to order, but living babies are born of sore travail and death agony. So revivals may be simulated, trumped up, made to order, but that is not how revivals begotten by the Holy Spirit come.

Three local leaders of The Salvation Army were concerned about the spiritual life of their corps (church). Souls were not being saved. They agreed to spend time in prayer. Saturday night they did not go home. Sunday they were not in the meetings. No one knew where they were. Sunday night there was a great "break" among the people in attendance. Many souls were at the penitent form (place at the altar for seeking forgiveness). Many tears were shed. All hearts seemed moved and softened. About ten o'clock at night, with tears streaming down their faces, these three leaders came from under the platform where they had spent Saturday night and all day Sunday in prayer. That was the secret of the great meeting.

Seventy years have passed over my head, fifty-seven of which I have spent in the service of my Lord, and forty-three with The Salvation Army. And the experience and observation of these years confirm me in my conviction that revivals are born, not made, and that God waits to be gracious and aid and answer prayer.

I experienced new life in Christ one Christmas Eve at the age of thirteen, and I have never looked back, though I sidestepped and faltered a bit at times in my early years. Immediately I joined the church, yielded loyally to its discipline, kept its rules, and though I didn't have the blessing of a clean heart I felt keenly that I must not prove false or do anything that would bring reproach upon the church or the cause of Christ. When I was fifteen years old, my mother slipped away to be with the Lord, and I became homeless for the next twelve years, with no one to counsel me, but this loyalty to the rules of the church safeguarded me.

For five years, I taught a Sunday school class, and at the age of twenty-three, I became a pastor, with four preaching places on my circuit, in three of which we had blazing revivals. Although I wasn't yet sanctified, I preached all the truth I knew with all my might, and believed what I preached with all my heart, and God blessed me, for He has always blessed and always will bless such preaching.

When He gloriously sanctified me, my knowledge and keen perception of truth were greatly enlarged and quickened, and my preaching became far more searching and effective. And now for forty-seven years God has been giving me revivals with many souls. This has been the glad and consuming ambition of my life. Place, promotion, power, and popularity have meant nothing to me compared with the smile of God and the winning of souls to Him. And this has enabled me to give myself wholly and effectively to my job without thought of what my job would give to me, and I shout "amen" to my Lord's word, "It is more blessed to give than to receive" (Acts 20:35 KJV).

Many kind and generous things have been said to me and about me, but the greatest compliment ever paid to me was by General William Booth, when, on two different occasions, he said to me, "Brengle, you are equal to your job," a job to which he appointed me, and in which he took special interest.[7] Since I knew his tongue was not that of an oily flatterer, and that he was not carrying flowers around for promiscuous presentation, I rejoiced, for one of my great desires was to gladden his heart, so often wounded, to put my full strength so far as possible under his vast burden, and to ease his anxieties where some others failed him.

The greatest compliment ever paid to my work was by Commissioner James Hay, following my seven months' campaign in Australia. He wrote the chief of staff,[8] saying that the campaign not only brought showers of blessing, but opened up spiritual springs. Showers are transient in effect, but springs flow on forever.

My father-in-law lived to be nearly ninety, and he said, "As men grow old they become either sweet or sour." He ripened sweetly and became more and more gracious in his old age. I want to be like that.

Let me grow lovely, growing old,

So many fine things do;

Laces, and ivory, and gold,

And silks need not be new;

And there is healing in old trees;

Old streets a glamour hold;

Why may not I, as well as these,

Grow lovely, growing old?[9]

Some painful and a few bitter things may have happened to me during these forty-three years I have been in The Salvation Army, but really I cannot recall them. I refuse to harbor such memories, so they fade away. Why should I pour bitter poison into the sweet wells of my joy, from which I must continue to drink if I would really live? I won't do it. Paul is my patron saint, and he has told me what to do: "Whatsoever things are true . . . honest . . . just . . . pure . . . lovely . . . of good report; if there be any virtue, and if there be any praise, think on these things" (Phil. 4:8 KJV). That I will, Paul.

At the same time, I do not want to indulge in saccharine sentimentality, for I remember that Jesus did not say, "You are the sugar of the earth" but "You are the salt of the earth" (Matt. 5:13 NLT). I must not lose my saltiness. But too much salt is dangerous, so I must beware. Nor must I ever forget, as our evangelist Paul bid me, to "patiently correct, rebuke, and encourage . . . people with good teaching. For a time is coming when people will no longer listen to sound and wholesome teaching. They will follow their own desires and will look for teachers who will tell them whatever their itching ears want to hear. They will reject the truth and chase after myths" (2 Tim. 4:2–4 NLT).

And though retired I must still "keep [my] head in all situations, endure hardship, do the work of an evangelist, discharge all the duties of [my] ministry" (2 Tim. 4:5 NIV). For the solemn day of accounting is yet to come—coming surely, swiftly—when I must render an account of my stewardship, when the final commendations or condemnations shall be spoken, when the great prizes and rewards will be given, and the awful deprivations and dooms will be announced.

Apostles though they were, Peter and Paul never lost their awe of that day. Nor must I, for Jesus said: "On judgment day many will say to me, 'Lord! Lord! We prophesied in your name and cast out demons in your name and performed many miracles in your name.' But I will reply, 'I never knew you. Get away from me, you who break God's laws'" (Matt. 7:22–23 NLT).

Remembering these words, I gird my armor closer, grip my sword, and—watching, praying, marching straight ahead—I sing:

My soul, be on thy guard!
Ten thousand foes arise;
The hosts of hell are pressing hard
To draw thee from the skies.

Ne'er think the battle won,
Nor lay thine armour down:
The fight of faith will not be done
Till thou obtain the crown![10]

It is a fight of faith, and faith is nourished by the Word of the Lord, to which I return daily for my portion and am not denied.

NOTES

1. Brengle attained his seventieth birthday in 1930.

2. George Heath, "My Soul, Be on Thy Guard," 1781, public domain.

3. Walter H. Brown, "O Little Mother of Mine," *The Labor Digest* 5, no. 1 (January 1912): 30.

4. Julia Ward Howe, "The Battle Hymn of the Republic," 1861, public domain.

5. Alfred Lord Tennyson, "In Memoriam," 1849, public domain.

6. Alfred Lord Tennyson, "Break, Break, Break," 1835, public domain.

7. The job here referred to is that of international evangelist for The Salvation Army.

8. The chief of staff is the second-in-command of the international Salvation Army.

9. Karle Wilson Baker, "Let Me Grow Lovely," 1923, public domain.

10. Heath, "My Soul, Be on Thy Guard."

Texts That Have Blessed Me 8

When I was a cadet in The Salvation Army's international training college forty-seven years ago, we had on the staff a young officer who had been a wild, reckless sinner. He had experienced new life in Christ only a short while when war broke out in Egypt and, being a military reservist, he was sent to the front. He had no Bible, and he could remember just one promise: "My grace is sufficient for you" (2 Cor. 12:9 NKJV).

In every temptation that assailed, every danger, every hour of spiritual loneliness, it was through this text that he looked up to God and claimed heavenly resources for his earthly needs. And he was not disappointed. His needs were met. God never failed him.

What a happy man to have such a promise! And yet how poor he was! He was like a beleaguered army with only one line of communication open, like a city with only one aqueduct for water or one dynamo for light, like a room with only one window or a house with just one door, like a car with one cylinder or a man with only one lung. There was only one star in his sky.

I remember how poor I felt him to be. He was not a juicy soul. He was not radiant. His face did not shine. It lacked solar light. I rejoiced that he was spiritually alive, but it was such an impoverished life! He was like a diver in the deep sea whose supply of oxygen came down through a pipeline, instead of being like a man on top of the world with all the winds blowing upon him, all the stars twinkling and dancing above him, all the glory of the cloudless days irradiating him.

When I am asked for my favorite Bible verse, I smile. It is not one text more than another, but *a whole Bible* that blesses, assures, warns, corrects, and comforts me. A hundred promises whisper to me. I never know when one of the promises—perhaps one that I have not met for days or even months—may suddenly stand before me, beckon me, speak to me tenderly, comfortingly, authoritatively, austerely, as though God were speaking to me face-to-face.

The ancient heroes of the cross obtained promises by faith. You can buy a Bible for a few dollars, and if you have not the money to buy, a Bible Society will give you one. And the Bible teems with promises. They are on almost every page. But your eyes will not see them, your mind will not grasp them, your heart will receive no strength and consolation from them, if you do not have faith. The person who goes through the Bible without faith is like those who walked over the diamond fields of Africa all unconscious of the immeasurable wealth beneath their feet.

When I say that I smile at being asked for my favorite promise and reply that it is the whole Bible which blesses me, I do not mean that there is no one promise that looms large to me, but rather that there are so many that bless me and meet my daily needs that I am like a man with a home full of sweet children, every one of whom is so dear to him that he cannot tell which he loves most and which is most needful for his happiness.

My spiritual needs are manifold, and there seems to be a promise just suited to my every need, that matches my need as a Yale key matches a Yale lock, as a glove fits the hand, as light answers to my eye and music to my ear, as the flavor of delicious food matches my sense of taste, and as the attar of roses answers my sense of smell, as the love of one's beloved and the faithfulness of one's friend answer the hunger of the heart.

For three or four years, I had known that someday I would have to come to close grips with myself and get the blessing of a clean heart if I was ever to see God in peace and have the power of the Holy Spirit in my life. At last I began to seek in earnest, and for three or four weeks I had become more and more hungry for the blessing. There were two things confronting me that I felt I could not do, but self had to be crucified. The way of faith was hidden from me because I hesitated to approach it by the way of wholehearted obedience.

But God was faithful. He did not leave me, but deepened conviction until I was in an agony. At last, at about nine o'clock on Friday morning, January 9, 1885, I could hold out no longer. My heart broke within me, and I yielded. Then instantly was whispered in my heart this text: "If we confess our sins, he is faithful and just to forgive us our sins, and to cleanse us from all unrighteousness" (1 John 1:9 KJV). The last part of the text was a revelation to me: "to cleanse us from all unrighteousness"—*all* unrighteousness.

I dropped my head in my hands and said, "Father, I believe that," and instantly peace passing all understanding flooded my soul, and I knew that I was clean. "The law of the Spirit of life in Christ Jesus" had "made me free from the law of sin and death" (Rom. 8:2 KJV).

Two days later I preached on the blessing and testified to it. But I trembled lest I might lose it. Then the Lord spoke to me in the words of Jesus to Martha, mourning over her dead brother, Lazarus: "I am the resurrection and the life. Anyone who believes in me will live, even after dying. Everyone who lives in me and believes in me will never ever die" (John 11:25–26 NLT).

Again I believed, and in that moment Christ was revealed in me as surely as He was revealed to Paul on the road to Damascus. I melted into tears and loved my Lord as I never dreamed one could love. Since then I have again and again cried out with Paul, "My old self has been crucified with Christ. It is no longer I who live, but Christ lives in me. So I live in this earthly body by trusting in the Son of God, who loved me and gave himself for me" (Gal. 2:20 NLT). And again and again I have said with Paul, "I once thought these things were valuable, but now I consider them worthless because of what Christ has done. Yes, everything else is worthless when compared with the infinite value of knowing Christ Jesus my Lord" (Phil. 3:7–8 NLT).

When again I feared lest I might fall, these two texts reassured me: "Don't be afraid, for I am with you. Don't be discouraged, for I am your God. I will strengthen you and help you. I will hold you up with my victorious right hand" (Isa. 41:10 NLT) and, "Now all glory to God, who is able to keep you from falling away and will bring you with great joy into his glorious presence without a single fault" (Jude 24 NLT).

Then I was tempted with the thought that, when I got old, the light would fade and the fire in my soul would go out. But these texts came with comforting assurance and power to my heart: "I will be your God throughout your lifetime—until your hair is white with age. I made you, and I will care for you. I will carry you along and save you" (Isa. 46:4 NLT) and, "The righteous . . . are planted in the house of the LORD; they flourish in the courts of our God. They still bear fruit in old age; they are ever full of sap and green" (Ps. 92:12–14 ESV).

I saw that I must not fear or be dismayed in the presence of any trouble or difficulty, but must quietly trust in the Lord. And I must not drift about as so many do, but remain "planted in the house of the LORD."

When I have gone to distant battlefields in far-off lands, among strangers, this promise has put comfort and strength into me: "My presence will go with you, and I will give you rest" (Ex. 33:14 ESV). And when I have felt any insufficiency I have been reassured with this promise: "Who makes a person's mouth? Who decides whether people speak or do not speak, hear or do not hear, see or do not see? Is it not I, the LORD? Now go! I will be with you as you speak, and I will instruct you in what to say" (Ex. 4:11–12 NLT).

These are only a few of a multitude of precious promises and words of the Lord which came to me years ago and which are ever whispering in my mind and heart, challenging my faith, my love, my utter devotion.

They are the joy and rejoicing of my heart, a heritage from the Lord, a lamp to my feet, a light to my path, a sword with which to thrust through the accusations and doubts and fears with which Satan is ever ready to assail me.

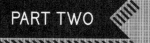

PART TWO

When the Holy Ghost Is Come

Who Is He? 1

On that last eventful evening in the upper room, just after the Passover Feast, Jesus spoke to His disciples about His departure. He commanded them to love one another. He told them not to be troubled in heart, but to hold fast their faith in Him. He assured them that though He was to die and leave them, He was going to the Father's many-mansioned house to prepare a place for them.

But already they were troubled, for what could this death and departure mean but the destruction of all their hopes, of all their cherished plans? Jesus had drawn them away from their fishing boats, their places of custom and daily employment, and inspired them with high personal and patriotic ambitions. He encouraged them to believe that He was the Seed of David, the promised Messiah, and they hoped that He would cast out Pilate and his hated Roman garrison, restore the kingdom to Israel, and sit on David's throne, a King, reigning in righteousness and undisputed power and majesty forever. And then, were they not to be His ministers of state and chief men in His kingdom?

He was their Leader, directing their labors. He was their Teacher, instructing their ignorance, solving their doubts and all their puzzling problems. He was their Defense, stilling the stormy sea and answering for them when questioned by wise and wily enemies.

They were poor and unlearned and weak. In Him was all their help, and what would they do—what could they do—without Him? They were without social standing, financial prestige, learning or intellectual equipment, political or military power. He was their all, and without Him they were as helpless as little children, as defenseless as lambs in the midst of wolves. How could their poor hearts be otherwise than troubled?

But then He gave them a strange, wonderful, and reassuring promise. He said, "If you love me, obey my commandments. And I will ask the Father, and he will give you another Advocate, who will never leave you" (John 14:15–16 NLT). I am going away, He said, but another shall come, who will fill My place. He shall not go away, but abide with you forever, and He "shall be in you" (John 14:17 KJV). And later He added, "It is expedient for you"—that is, better for you—"that I go away: for if I go not away, the Comforter will not come" (John 16:7 KJV).

Who is this other One—this Comforter? He must be some august Divine Person, and not a mere influence or impersonal force, for how else could He take and fill the place of Jesus? How else could it be said that it was better to have Him than to have Jesus remaining in the flesh? He must be strong and wise, and tender and true, to take the place of the Blessed One who was to die and depart. Who is He?

John, writing in the Greek language, called Him *Paraclete*, but we in English call Him "Comforter." But *Paraclete* means more—much more—than *Comforter*. It means "one called in to help: an advocate, a helper." The same word is used of Jesus in 1 John 2:1: "We have an advocate"—a Paraclete, a Helper—"with the Father, Jesus Christ the righteous" (KJV). Just as Jesus had gone to be the disciples' Advocate, their Helper, in the heavens, so this other Paraclete was to be their Advocate, their Helper, on earth. He would be their Comforter when comfort was needed, but He would be more. He would also be their Teacher, Guide, and Strengthener, as Jesus had been. At every point of need He would be there as an ever-present, all-wise, and almighty Helper. He would meet their need with His sufficiency, their weakness with His strength, their foolishness with His wisdom, their ignorance with His knowledge, and their blindness and shortsightedness with His perfect, all-embracing vision. What a Comforter! Why should they be troubled?

They were weak, but He would strengthen them with might in their inner beings (see Eph. 3:16). They were to give the world the words of Jesus and teach all nations (see Matt. 28:19–20), and He would teach them all things and bring to their remembrance all Jesus had said to them (see John 14:26).

They were to guide new believers in the right way, and He was to guide them into all truth (see John 16:13). They were to attack hoary systems of evil and inbred and actively entrenched sin in every human heart, but He was to go before them, preparing the way for conquest by convincing the world of sin, of righteousness, and of judgment (see John 16:8). They were to bear heavy burdens and face superhuman tasks, but He was to give them power (see Acts 1:8). Indeed, He was to be a Comforter, Strengthener, and Helper.

Jesus had been external to them. They often missed Him. Sometimes He was asleep when they felt they sorely needed Him. Sometimes He was on the mountains while they were in the valley vainly trying to cast out stubborn devils or wearily toiling on the tumultuous, wind-tossed sea. Sometimes He was surrounded by vast crowds, and He entered into high disputes with the doctors of the law, and they had to wait until He was alone to seek explanations of His teachings. But they were never to lose this other Helper in the crowd nor be separated for an instant from Him, for no human being, nor untoward circumstance, nor physical necessity, could ever come between Him and them, for, as Jesus said, He "shall be in you" (John 14:17 KJV).

From the words used to declare the sayings, the doings, the offices, and the works of the Comforter, the Holy Spirit, we are forced to conclude that He is a Divine Person. Out of the multitude of Scriptures that could be quoted, note this passage, which (as nearly as is possible with human language) reveals to us His personality: "Now there were in the church at Antioch prophets and teachers, Barnabas, Simeon who was called Niger, Lucius of Cyrene, Manaen a lifelong friend of Herod the tetrarch, and Saul. While they were worshiping the Lord and fasting, the Holy Spirit said, 'Set apart for me Barnabas and Saul for the work to which I have called them.' Then after fasting and praying they laid their hands on them and sent them off. So, being sent out by the Holy Spirit, they went down to Seleucia" (Acts 13:1–4 ESV).

Further on we read that they were "forbidden by the Holy Spirit to speak the word in Asia," and when they would have gone into Bithynia, the Spirit "did not allow them" (Acts 16:6–7 ESV).

Later, when the messengers of Cornelius, the Roman centurion, were seeking Peter, "the Holy Spirit said to him, 'Three men have come looking for you. Get up, go downstairs, and go with them without hesitation. Don't worry, for I have sent them'" (Acts 10:19–20 NLT).

These are just a few of the passages of Scripture that might be quoted to establish the fact of His personality—His power to think, will, act, and speak. And if His personality is not made plain in these Scriptures, then it is impossible for human language to make it so.

Indeed, I am persuaded that if an intelligent person who had never seen the Bible should for the first time read the four gospels and the Acts of the apostles, he or she would say that the personality of the Holy Spirit is as clearly revealed in Acts as is the personality of Jesus Christ in the Gospels. In truth, the Acts of the apostles are in a large measure the acts of the Holy Spirit, and the disciples were not more certainly under the immediate direction of Jesus during the three years of His earthly ministry than they were under the direct leadership of the Spirit after Pentecost.

But there are those who admit His personality yet (in their loyalty to the divine unity) deny the Trinity, and maintain that the Holy Spirit is only the Father manifesting Himself as Spirit, without any distinction in personality. But this view cannot be harmonized with certain Scriptures. While the Bible and reason plainly declare that there is but one God, the Scriptures just as clearly reveal that there are three persons in the Godhead: Father, Son, and Holy Spirit.

The form of Paul's benediction to the Corinthians proves the doctrine: "May the grace of the Lord Jesus Christ, the love of God, and the fellowship of the Holy Spirit be with you all" (2 Cor. 13:14 NLT).

Again, it is taught in the promise of Jesus, already quoted, "I will ask the Father, and he will give you another Advocate, who will never leave you" (John 14:15–16 NLT). Here the three persons of the Godhead are clearly revealed. The Son prays, the Father answers, and the Spirit comes.

The Holy Spirit is "another Comforter," a second Comforter succeeding the first (who was Jesus), and both were given by the Father.

Do you say, "I cannot understand it"? Neither do I. Who *can* understand it? God does not expect us to understand it. Nor would He have us puzzle our heads and trouble our hearts in attempting to understand it or harmonize it with our knowledge of arithmetic. It is only the fact that is revealed; *how* there can be three persons in one Godhead is not revealed.

The how is a mystery, and is not a matter of faith at all. But the fact is a matter of revelation, and therefore a matter of faith. I myself am a mysterious trinity of body, mind, and spirit. The fact I believe, but the how is not a thing to believe. It is at this point that many puzzle and perplex themselves needlessly.

In the ordinary affairs of life, we grasp facts and hold them fast without puzzling ourselves over the "how" of things. Who can explain how food sustains life, how light reveals material objects, or how sound conveys ideas to our minds? It is the fact we know and believe, but the "how" we pass by as a mystery unrevealed. What God has revealed, we believe. We cannot understand how Jesus turned water into wine, how He multiplied a few loaves and fishes and fed thousands, how He stilled the stormy sea, how He opened blind eyes, how He healed lepers, and how He raised the dead by a word. But the facts we believe. Wireless telegraphic messages are sent over the vast wastes of ocean. That is a fact, and we believe it. But how they go we do not know. That is not something to believe.

An old servant of God has pointed out that it is the *fact* of the Trinity—and not the *manner* of it—which God has revealed and made a subject for our faith.

But while the Scriptures reveal to us the fact of the personality of the Holy Spirit, and it is a subject for our faith, to those in whom He dwells this fact may become a matter of sacred knowledge, of blessed experience.

How else can we account for the positive and assured way in which the apostles and other disciples spoke of the Holy Spirit on and after the day of Pentecost, if they did not know Him? Immediately after the fiery baptism, with its blessed filling, Peter stood before the people and said, "[This] was predicted long ago by the prophet Joel: 'In the last days,' God says, 'I will pour out my Spirit upon all people'" (Acts 2:16–17 NLT). Then he exhorted the people and assured them that if they would meet certain simple conditions they would "receive the gift of the Holy Spirit" (Acts 2:38 NLT). He said to Ananias, "Why has Satan filled your heart to lie to the Holy Spirit?" (Acts 5:3 ESV). He declared to the high priest and council that he and his fellow apostles were witnesses of the resurrection of Jesus, and added, "And so is the Holy Spirit, who is given by God to those who obey him" (Acts 5:32 NLT). Without any apology, explanation, "think so," or "hope so," they spoke of being "filled," not simply with some new, strange experience or emotion, but "with the Holy Spirit" (Acts 9:17 NLT). Certainly they must have known Him. And if they knew Him, may we not know Him also?

Paul said, "And we have received God's Spirit (not the world's spirit), so we can know the wonderful things God has freely given us. When we tell you these things, we do not use words that come from human wisdom. Instead, we speak words given to us by the Spirit, using the Spirit's words to explain spiritual truths" (1 Cor. 2:12–13 NLT). And if we know the words, may we not know the Teacher of the words?

John Wesley wrote:

The knowledge of the Three-One God is interwoven with all true Christian faith; with all vital religion.

I do not say that every real Christian can say with the Marquis de Renty, "I bear about with me continually an experimental verity, and a plenitude of the presence of the ever blessed Trinity." I apprehend that this is not the experience of "babes," but rather "fathers in Christ."

But I know not how anyone can be a Christian believer, till he "hath [as St. John speaks] the witness in himself"; till "the Spirit of God witnesses with his spirit, that he is a child of God"; that is, in effect, till God the Holy Ghost witnesses that God the Father has accepted him through the merits of God the Son. . . .

Not that every Christian believer *adverts* to this; perhaps, at first, not one in twenty: but if you ask any of them a few questions, you will easily find it is implied in what he believes.[1]

I shall never forget my joy, mingled with awe and wonder, when this dawned upon my consciousness. For several weeks I had been searching the Scriptures, ransacking my heart, humbling my soul, and crying to God almost day and night for a pure heart and the baptism with the Holy Spirit, when one glad, sweet day—it was January 9, 1885—this text suddenly opened to my understanding: "If we confess our sins, he is faithful and just to forgive us our sins, and to cleanse us from all unrighteousness" (1 John 1:9 KJV). And I was enabled to believe without any doubt that the precious blood cleansed my heart, even mine, from all sin. Shortly after that, while reading these words of Jesus to Martha—"I am the resurrection and the life. Anyone who believes in me will live, even after dying. Everyone who lives in me and believes in me will never ever die" (John 11:25–26 NLT)—instantly my heart was melted like wax before fire. Jesus Christ was revealed to my spiritual consciousness, revealed in me, and my soul was filled with unutterable love. I walked in a heaven of love. Then one day, with amazement, I said to a friend, "This is the perfect love about which the apostle John wrote, but it is beyond all I dreamed of. In it is personality. His love thinks, wills, talks with me, corrects me, instructs and teaches me." And then I knew that God the Holy Spirit was in this love, and that this love was God, for "God is love" (1 John 4:8 KJV).

Oh, the rapture mingled with reverential, holy fear—for it is a rapturous, yet divinely fearful thing—to be indwelt by the Holy Spirit, to be a temple of the living God! Great heights are always opposite great depths, and from the heights of this blessed experience many have plunged into the dark depths of fanaticism. But we must not draw back from the experience through fear. All danger will be avoided by meekness and lowliness of heart; by humble, faithful service; by esteeming others better than ourselves and in honor preferring them before ourselves; by keeping an open, teachable spirit—in a word, by looking steadily unto Jesus, to whom the Holy Spirit continually points us. For He would not have us fix our attention exclusively upon Himself and His work in us, but also upon the Crucified One and His work for us, that we may walk in the steps of Him whose blood purchases our pardon and makes and keeps us clean.

Great Paraclete! To Thee we cry:
O highest gift of God most high!
O fount of life! O fire of love!
And sweet anointing from above!

Our senses touch with light and fire;
Our hearts with tender love inspire;
And with endurance from on high
The weakness of our flesh supply.

Far back our Enemy repel,
And let Thy peace within us dwell;
So may we, having Thee for Guide,
Turn from each hurtful thing aside.

Oh, may Thy grace on us bestow
The Father and the Son to know,
And evermore to hold confessed
Thyself of each the Spirit blest.[2]

NOTES

1. John Wesley, *The Works of the Reverend John Wesley, A. M.*, vol. 2 (New York: J. Emory and B. Waugh, 1831), 24.

2. Rabanus Maurus, "Veni Creator Spiritus," trans. Robert Bridges, n. d., public domain.

Preparing His House 2

Jesus said, "I assure you, no one can enter the Kingdom of God without being born of water and the Spirit. Humans can reproduce only human life, but the Holy Spirit gives birth to spiritual life" (John 3:5–6 NLT). And Paul wrote to the Romans, "Those who do not have the Spirit of Christ living in them do not belong to him at all" (Rom. 8:9 NLT).

So it must be that all children of God, all true followers of Jesus, have the Holy Spirit in some gracious manner and measure, or else they would not be children of God, for only those "who are led by the Spirit of God are children of God" (Rom. 8:14 NLT).

It is the Holy Spirit who convicts us of sin, who makes us feel how good and righteous, just and patient God is—and how guilty we are, how unfit for heaven, and how near to hell. It is the Holy Spirit who leads us to true repentance and confession and amendment of life.

And when our repentance is complete and our surrender is uncondi-
tional, it is He who reasons with us, calms our fears, soothes our troubled hearts, banishes our darkness, and enables us to look to Jesus and
believe in Him for the forgiveness of all our sins and the salvation of
our souls. And when we yield and trust, and are accepted by the Lord
and saved by grace, it is He who assures us of the Father's favor and
notifies us that we are now His. "For his Spirit joins with our spirit to
affirm that we are God's children" (Rom. 8:16 NLT). He is "the Spirit
of adoption by whom we cry out, 'Abba, Father'" (Rom. 8:15 NKJV).

> And His that gentle voice we hear,
> Soft as the breath of even;
> That checks each thought, that calms each fear,
> And speaks of heaven.[1]

It is He who strengthens new Christians to fight against and overcome sin, and it is He who engenders within them a hope of fuller
righteousness through faith in Christ.

> And every virtue we possess,
> And every victory won,
> And every thought of holiness,
> Are His alone.[2]

But great and gracious as this work is, it is not the fiery baptism
with the Spirit that is promised. It is not the fullness of the Holy Spirit
to which we are exhorted. This is only the initial work of the Spirit.

It is only the clear dawn of the day, and not the rising of the daystar. It is perfect of its kind, but it is preparatory to another and fuller work. Jesus said to His earliest disciples, concerning the Holy Spirit, that "the world [those who have not yet experienced new life in Christ] cannot receive him, because it isn't looking for him and doesn't recognize him" (John 14:17 NLT). They resist Him and will not permit Him to work in their hearts. Then Jesus added, "But you know him, because he lives with you now." He had begun His work in them, but there was more to follow, for Jesus said, "And later [He] will be in you" (John 14:17 NLT).

If you were to build yourself a house, you would be in and out of it and all around it. But we would not say you live in it until it has been completed. It is in that sense that Jesus said, "He lives with you." But when the house is finished, you sweep out all the chips and sawdust, scrub the floor, lay down the carpets, hang up your pictures, arrange the furniture, and move in with your family. Then you are in the fullest sense within it. You abide there. And it is in that sense that Jesus meant that the Holy Spirit would be in His followers. This is fitly expressed in the chorus:

> Holy Spirit, come, O come!
> Let Thy work in me be done!
> All that hinders shall be thrown aside;
> Make me fit to be Thy dwelling.[3]

Previous to the day of Pentecost, the Holy Spirit was with those first disciples, using the searching preaching of John the Baptist and the life, words, example, sufferings, death, and resurrection of Jesus as instruments with which to fashion their hearts for His indwelling. As the truth was declared to them in the words of Jesus, pictured to them in His actions, exemplified in His daily life, and fulfilled in His death and His rising from the dead, the Holy Spirit worked mightily within them. But He could not yet find perfect rest in their hearts, and so He did not yet abide within them.

They had forsaken all to follow Christ. They had been commissioned to preach the gospel, heal the sick, cleanse the lepers, raise the dead, and cast out devils. Their names were written in heaven. They were not of the world, even as Jesus was not of the world, for they belonged to Him and to the Father. They knew the Holy Spirit, for He was with them and working in them, but He was not yet living in them, for they were still carnal. That is, they were selfish, each seeking the best place for himself. They disputed among themselves as to whom should be the greatest. They were bigoted, wanting to call down fire from heaven to consume those who would not receive Jesus and forbidding those who would not follow them to cast out devils in His name. They were positive and loud in their professions of devotion and loyalty to Jesus when alone with Him—they declared they would die with Him—but they were fearful, timid, and false to Him when the testing time came. When the mocking crowd appeared, and danger was near, they all forsook Him and fled, while Peter cursed and swore and denied that he knew Him.

But the Holy Spirit did not forsake them. He still worked within them, and no doubt used their very mistakes and miserable failures to perfect within them the spirit of humility and perfect self-abasement in order that they might safely be exalted. And on the day of Pentecost His work of preparation was complete, and He moved in to abide forever.

And this experience of theirs before Pentecost is the common experience of all believers. Every child of God knows that the Holy Spirit is with him or her, and realizes that He is working within, striving to set the house in order. And with many who are properly taught and gladly obedient, this work is done quickly, and the heavenly Dove, the Blessed One, takes up His constant abode within them. The toil and strife with inbred sin is ended by its destruction, and they enter at once into the Sabbath of full salvation.

Surely this is possible. The disciples could not receive the Holy Spirit until Jesus was glorified, because the foundation for perfect, intelligent, unwavering faith was not laid until then. But since the day of Pentecost, He may be received immediately by those who have repented of all sin, believed in Jesus, and been born again. Some have assured me that they were sanctified wholly and filled with the Spirit within a few hours of their new birth in Christ. I have no doubt that this was so with many of the three thousand who experienced new life in Christ as a result of Peter's preaching on the day of Pentecost.

But often this work is slow, for He can work effectually only as we work with Him, practicing intelligent and obedient faith. Some days the work prospers and seems almost complete, and then peace and joy and comfort abound in the heart. At other times the work is hindered, and often almost undone by the strivings and stirrings of inbred sin, fits of temper, lightness and frivolity, worldliness, unholy ambitions, jealousies and envying, uncharitable suspicions and harsh judgments and selfish indulgences, slowness to believe, and neglect of watchfulness and prayer and the patient, attentive study of His Word.

"The desires of the flesh are against the Spirit" (Gal. 5:17 ESV), seeking to bring the soul back under the bondage of sin again, while the Spirit wars against the flesh, which is "the old, sinful nature." The Spirit seeks to bring every thought "into captivity to the obedience of Christ" (2 Cor. 10:5 NKJV), to lead the soul to that point of glad, whole-hearted consecration to its Lord, and that simple, perfect faith in the merits of His blood which shall enable Him to cast out and destroy the old, sinful nature and, making the heart His temple, enthrone Christ within.

> Here on earth a temple stands,
>
> Temple never built with hands;
>
> There the Lord doth fill the place
>
> With the glory of His grace.
>
> Cleansed by Christ's atoning blood,
>
> Thou art this fair house of God.
>
> Thoughts, desires, that enter there,
>
> Should they not be pure and fair?
>
> Meet for holy courts and blest,
>
> Courts of stillness and of rest,
>
> Where the soul, a priest in white,
>
> Singeth praises day and night;
>
> Glory of the love divine,
>
> Filling all this heart of mine.[4]

What is your experience? Are you filled with the Spirit? Or is the old, sinful nature still warring against Him in your heart? Oh, that you may receive Him fully by faith right now!

NOTES

1. Harriet Auber, "Our Blest Redeemer, Ere He Breathed," 1829, public domain.

2. Ibid.

3. Richard Slater, "All the Guilty Past Is Washed Away," *The Salvation Army Songbook*, n. d., public domain.

4. Gerhard Tersteegan, "Here on Earth a Temple Stands," trans. Emma Frances Shuttleworth Bevan, 1731, public domain.

Is the Baptism with the Holy Spirit a Third Blessing?

There is much difference of opinion among many of God's children as to the time and order of the baptism with the Holy Spirit. And many who believe that entire cleansing is subsequent to salvation ask if the baptism with the Spirit is not subsequent to cleansing, and therefore a third blessing.

There are four types of teachers whose views appear to differ about this subject.

1. Those who emphasize cleansing, who say much of a clean heart but little, if anything, about the fullness of the Holy Spirit and power from on high.

2. Those who emphasize the baptism with the Holy Spirit and fullness of the Spirit, but say little or nothing of cleansing from inbred sin and the destruction of the carnal mind.

3. Those who say much of both but separate them into two distinct experiences, often widely separated in time.

4. Those who teach that the truth is in the union of the two and that, while we may separate them in their order (putting cleansing first), we cannot separate them in time. They cannot be separated since it is the baptism that cleanses, just as the darkness vanishes before the flash of the electric light when the right button is touched, just as the Augean stables in the fabled story of Grecian mythology were cleansed when Hercules turned in the floods of the River Arno and the refuse went out as the rushing waters poured in.

However, in John 17, Jesus prayed for His disciples, and said,

I'm not asking you to take them out of the world, but to keep them safe from the evil one. . . . Make them holy . . . that they will all be one, just as you and I are one—as you are in me, Father, and I am in you. And may they be in us. . . . I am in them and you are in me. May they experience such perfect unity. . . . Then your love for me will be in them, and I will be in them. (John 17:15, 17, 21, 23, 26 NLT)

It is first sanctification (cleansing, being made holy) then filling (divine union with the Father and the Son through the Holy Spirit). The Scriptures make plain the order of God's work, and if we looked at them alone, without diligently comparing Scripture with Scripture as God would have us do, we might conclude that the cleansing and filling were as distinct and separate in time as they are in this order of statement.

But other Scriptures give us abundant light on that side of the subject. In Acts 10:44, we read of Peter's preaching Jesus to Cornelius, the Roman centurion, and his household, and "even as Peter was saying these things, the Holy Spirit fell upon all who were listening to the message" (NLT). And in Acts 15:7–9, at the first Council of Jerusalem, we have Peter's rehearsal of the experience of Cornelius and his household: "At the meeting, after a long discussion, Peter stood and addressed them as follows: 'Brothers, you all know that God chose me from among you some time ago to preach to the Gentiles so that they could hear the Good News and believe. God knows people's hearts, and he confirmed that he accepts Gentiles by giving them the Holy Spirit, just as he did to us. He made no distinction between us and them, for he cleansed their hearts through faith.'" (Acts 15:7–9 NLT).

Here we see that their believing and the sudden descent of the Holy Spirit with cleansing power into their hearts constitute one blessed experience.

What patient, waiting, expectant faith reckons done, the baptism with the Holy Spirit actually accomplishes. There may be an interval of time between the act of faith by which a person begins to reckon him- or herself "dead indeed unto sin, but alive unto God through Jesus Christ our Lord" (Rom. 6:11 KJV) and the act of the Holy Spirit which makes the reckoning good. But the act and state of steadfastly, patiently, joyously, perfectly believing (which is our part) and the act of baptizing with the Holy Spirit, cleansing as by fire (which is God's part) bring about the one experience of entire sanctification. These must not and cannot be logically looked upon as two distinct blessings any more than the act of the husband and the act of the wife can be separated in the one experience of marriage.

There are two works and two workers—God and us—just as my right arm and my left arm work when my two hands come together but the union of the two hands constitutes one experience.

If my left arm acts quickly, my right arm will surely respond. And so, if the soul, renouncing self and sin and the world, with ardor of faith in the precious blood for cleansing and in the promise of the gift of the Holy Spirit, draws near to God, God will draw near to that soul, and the blessed union will be effected suddenly. In that instant, what faith has reckoned done will be done; the death stroke will be given to the old, sinful nature; sin will die; and the heart will be clean indeed and wholly alive toward God through our Lord Jesus Christ. It will not be a mere "make believe" experience, but a gloriously real one.

It is possible that some have been led into confusion on this subject by not considering all the Scriptures bearing on it. What is it that cleanses or sanctifies, and how? Jesus prayed, "Sanctify them by Your truth. Your word is truth" (John 17:17 NKJV). Here it is the Word, or truth, that sanctifies.

John said, "The blood of Jesus, his Son, cleanses us from all sin" (1 John 1:7 NLT). Here it is the blood.

Peter said, "[God] put no difference between us and them, purifying their hearts by faith" (Acts 15:9 KJV). And Paul said, "That they may receive forgiveness of sins, and inheritance among them which are sanctified by faith" (Acts 26:18 KJV). Here it is by faith.

Paul also wrote, "God chose you to be among the first to experience salvation—a salvation that came through the Spirit who makes you holy and through your belief in the truth" (2 Thess. 2:13 NLT). And again, "I bring you the Good News so that I might present you as an acceptable offering to God, made holy by the Holy Spirit" (Rom. 15:16 NLT). And Peter wrote, "God the Father knew you and chose you long ago, and his Spirit has made you holy" (1 Pet. 1:2 NLT). Here it is the Spirit that sanctifies or makes clean and holy.

Is there confusion then? Jesus said, "The truth." John said, "The blood." Paul and Peter said, "Faith" and "the Holy Spirit." Can these be reconciled? Let us see.

Picture a child in a burning house. A man risks his life and rushes to the spot above which the child stands in awful danger, and cries out, "Jump, and I will catch you!" The child hears, believes, leaps, and the man receives him. But just as he turns and places the boy in safety, a falling timber strikes him to the ground, wounded to death, and his flowing blood sprinkles the boy whom he has saved.

A breathless spectator says, "The child's faith saved him." Another says, "How quick the lad was! His courageous leap saved him." Another says, "Bless the child! He was in awful danger, and he just barely saved himself." Another says, "That man's word just reached the boy's ear in the nick of time, and saved him." Another says, "God bless that man! He saved that child." And yet another says, "That boy was saved by blood—by the sacrifice of that heroic man!"

What saved the child? Without the man's presence and promise there would have been no faith. And without faith there would have been no saving action and the boy would have perished. The man's word saved him by inspiring faith. Faith saved him by leading to proper action. He saved himself by leaping. The man saved him by sacrificing his own life in order to catch him when he leaped.

Not the child himself alone, nor his faith, nor his brave leap, nor his rescuer's word, nor his blood, nor the man himself saved the boy, but they all together saved him. And the boy was not saved until he was in the arms of the man.

So it is faith and works—and the Word and the blood and the Holy Spirit—that sanctify.

The blood, the sacrifice of Christ, underlies all, and is the meritorious cause of every blessing we receive, but the Holy Spirit is the active agent by whom the merits of the blood are applied to our needs.

During the American Civil War, certain men committed some shameful and unlawful deeds and were sentenced to be shot. On the day of the execution, they stood in a row confronted by soldiers with loaded muskets, waiting the command to fire. Just before the command was given, the commanding officer felt a touch on his elbow and, turning, saw a young man by his side, who said, "Sir, there in that row, waiting to be shot, is a married man. He has a wife and children. He is their breadwinner. If you shoot him, he will be sorely missed. Let me take his place."

"All right," said the officer. "Take his place, if you wish. But you will be shot."

"I quite understand that," replied the young man, "but no one will miss me." He went to the condemned man, pushed him aside, and took his place.

Soon the command to fire was given. The volley rang out, and the young hero dropped dead with a bullet through his heart while the other man went free.

His freedom came to him by blood. However, had he neglected the great salvation and—despising the blood shed for him and refusing the sacrifice of the friend and the righteous claims of the law—persisted in the same evil ways, he too would have been shot. The blood, though shed for him, would not have availed to set him free. But he accepted the sacrifice, submitted to the law, and went home to his wife and children. It was by the blood. Every breath he henceforth drew, every throb of his heart, every blessing he enjoyed or possibly could enjoy, came to him by the blood. He owed everything from that day forth to the blood, and every fleeting moment, every passing day, and every rolling year but increased his debt to the blood that had been shed for him.

And so we owe all to the blood of Christ, for we were under sentence of death—"The soul who sins shall die" (Ezek. 18:20 NKJV), and we have all sinned. And God, to be holy, must frown upon sin and utterly condemn it, and must execute His sentence against it.

But Jesus suffered for our sins. He died for us. "He was wounded for our transgressions, he was bruised for our iniquities . . . and with his stripes we are healed" (Isa. 53:5 KJV). "For you know that God paid a ransom to rescue you from the empty life you inherited from your ancestors. And it was not paid with mere gold or silver. . . . It was the precious blood of Christ," who loved you and gave Himself for you (1 Pet. 1:18–19 NLT; see also Gal. 2:20). And now every blessing we ever had, or ever shall have, comes to us by the divine sacrifice, by "the precious blood." And "how shall we escape, if we neglect so great salvation" (Heb. 2:3 KJV)? His blood is the meritorious cause not only of our pardon, but also of our cleansing, our sanctification. But the Holy Spirit is the ever-present, living, active cause.

The truth or Word that sanctifies is the record God has given us of His will and of that divine sacrifice, that "precious blood." The faith that purifies is the sure confidence in that Word which leads to renunciation of all self-righteousness, utter abandonment to God's will, full dependence on the merits of the precious blood, and "faith expressing itself in love" (Gal. 5:6 NLT), for "faith without works is dead" (James 2:20 KJV). And thus we draw near to God, God draws near to us, and the Holy Spirit falls upon us, comes into us, and cleanses our hearts by the destruction of sin and the infilling of God's love.

The advocates of entire sanctification as an experience wrought in the soul by the baptism with the Spirit subsequent to regeneration call it "the second blessing." But many good people object to the term and say that they have received the first, second, third, and fiftieth blessing. No doubt they have. But the people who speak of "the second blessing" are right in the sense in which they use the term. In that sense there are only the two blessings.

Some years ago a man heard things about a lady that filled him with admiration for her and made him feel that they were of one mind and heart. Later he met her for the first time and fell in love with her. After some months, following an enlarged acquaintance and much consideration and prayer, he told her of his love and asked her to become his wife. After due consideration and prayer on her part she consented, and they promised themselves to each other and in a sense gave themselves to each other.

That was the first blessing, and it filled him with great peace and joy, but not perfect peace and joy. And there were many blessings following that. Every letter he received, every tender look, every pressure of the hand, every tone of her voice, every fresh assurance of enduring and increasing affection was a blessing. But it was not the second blessing.

Then one day, after patient waiting and full preparation, they came together in the presence of friends and before a representative of God, and in the most solemn and irrevocable manner gave themselves to each other to become one and were pronounced husband and wife. That was the second blessing, an epochal experience, unlike anything which preceded or anything to follow. And now their peace and joy and rest were full.

There had to be the first and second blessings in this relationship of husband and wife, but there is no third. And yet in the sense of those who say they have received fifty blessings from the Lord, there have been countless blessings in their wedded life. Indeed, it has been a river of blessing, broadening and deepening in gladness, joy, sweet affections, and fellowship with the increasing years.

But let us not confuse things by disputing over terms and wrangling about words. The first blessing in Jesus Christ is salvation, with its negative side of remission of sins and forgiveness, and its positive side of renewal or regeneration—the new birth—one experience.

The second blessing is entire sanctification, with its negative side of cleansing and its positive side of filling with the Holy Spirit—one whole, rounded, glorious, epochal experience. And while there may subsequently be many refreshings, girdings, illuminations, and secret tokens and assurances of love and favor, there is no third blessing in this large sense, in this present time. But when time is no more, when the everlasting doors have lifted up and the King of Glory comes in with His bride, and He makes us, forever redeemed and crowned, to sit down with Him on His throne, then in eternity we shall have the third blessing—we shall be glorified.

The Witness of the Spirit 4

How shall I know that I am accepted by God—that I am saved or sanctified? The Bible declares God's love and pity for sinners, including me, and reveals His offer of mercy to me in Jesus Christ, on condition that I fully repent of my sins and, yielding myself to Him, believe in Jesus Christ, take up my cross, and follow Him. But how shall I know that I have met these conditions in a way to satisfy Him?

The Bible cannot tell me this. It tells me what to do, but it does not tell me when I have done it, any more than the sign at the country crossroads, pointing out the road leading to the city, tells me when I have arrived at the city.

My religious teachers and friends cannot tell me, for they cannot read my heart, nor the mind of God toward me. How can they know when I have in my heart repented and believed, and when His righteous anger is turned away? They can encourage me to repent, believe, and obey. They can assure me that if I do, He will accept me, and I shall be a new creation. But beyond that they cannot.

My own heart, owing to its darkness, deceitfulness, and liability to error, is not a safe witness previous to the assurance God Himself gives. If my neighbor is justly offended with me, it is not my own heart, but his testimony that first assures me of his favor once more.

How, then, shall I know that I am justified or wholly sanctified? There is only one way, and that is by the witness of the Holy Spirit. God must notify me and make me to know it. And this He does when, despairing of my own works of righteousness, I cast my poor soul fully and in faith upon Jesus. "For you did not receive a spirit of slavery to fall back into fear," said Paul, "but you have received the Spirit of adoption as sons, by whom we cry, 'Abba! Father!' The Spirit himself bears witness with our spirit that we are children of God" (Rom. 8:15–16 ESV). "And because we are his children, God has sent the Spirit of his Son into our hearts, prompting us to call out, 'Abba, Father'" (Gal. 4:6 NLT). Unless He Himself assures me, I shall never know that He accepts me, but must continue in uncertainty all my days.

> Come, Holy Ghost, Thyself impress
> On my expanding heart:
> And show that in the Father's grace
> I share a filial part.[1]

William Booth said, "Assurance is produced by the revelation of forgiveness and acceptance made by God Himself directly to the soul. This is the witness of the Spirit. It is God testifying in my soul that He has loved me, and given Himself for me, and washed me from my sins in His own blood. Nothing short of this actual revelation, made by God Himself, can make anyone sure of salvation."[2]

John Wesley said, "By the testimony of the Spirit, I mean an inward impression of the soul, whereby the Spirit of God immediately and directly witnesses to my spirit that I am a child of God; that 'Jesus hath loved me, and given himself for me'; that all my sins are blotted out, and I, even I, am reconciled to God."[3]

This witness of the Spirit addressed to my consciousness enables me to sing with joyful assurance,

> My God is reconciled;
> His pardoning voice I hear:
> He owns me for His child;
> I can no longer fear:
> With confidence I now draw nigh,
> And, "Father, Abba, Father," cry.[4]

When the Holy Spirit witnesses to me that I am saved and adopted into God's family as His child, then other evidences begin to abound also. For instance:

1. My own spirit witnesses that I am a new creature. I know that old things have passed away and all things have become new. My very thoughts and desires have been changed. Love and joy and peace reign within me. My heart no longer condemns me. Pride, selfishness, lust, and temper no longer control my thoughts nor lead captive my will. I infer without doubt that this is God's work in me.

2. My conscience bears witness that I am honest and true in all my purposes and intentions, that I am without guile, that my eye is focused only on the glory of God, and that with all simplicity and sincerity of heart I serve Him. And, since by nature I am only sinful, I again infer that this sincerity of heart is His blessed work in my soul and is a fruit of salvation.

3. The Bible becomes a witness to my salvation. In it are accurately portrayed the true characteristics of the children of God, and as I study it prayerfully and find these characteristics in my heart and life, I again infer that I am God's child. This is true self-examination, and is most useful.

These evidences are most important to guard us against any mistake as to the witness of the Holy Spirit.

The witness of the Spirit is not likely to be mistaken for something else, just as the sun is not likely to be mistaken for a lesser light—a glowworm or a moon. But one who has not seen the sun might mistake some lesser light for the sun. So those who have not truly experienced new life in Christ may mistake some flash of fancy or some pleasant emotion for the witness of the Spirit. But if they are honest, the absence of these secondary evidences and witnesses will correct them. They must know that so long as sin masters them and reigns within them, and they are devoid of the tempers, graces, and dispositions of God's people as portrayed in the Bible, that they are mistaken in supposing that they have the witness of the Spirit. The Holy Spirit cannot witness to what does not exist. He cannot lie. Not until sin is forgiven does He witness to the fact. Not until we are justified from our old sins and born again does He witness that we are children of

God. And when He does so witness, these secondary evidences always follow. Charles Wesley expresses this in one of his matchless hymns:

> How can a sinner know
> His sins on earth forgiven?
> How can my gracious Savior show
> My name inscribed in heaven?

> We who in Christ believe
> That He for us hath died,
> We all His unknown peace receive,
> And feel His blood applied.

> His love, surpassing far
> The love of all beneath,
> We find within our hearts, and dare
> The pointless darts of death.

> Stronger than death and hell
> The mystic power we prove;
> And conquerors of the world, we dwell
> In heaven, who dwell in love.[5]

The witness of the Spirit is far more comprehensive than many suppose. Multitudes do not believe there is any such thing, while others confine it to the forgiveness of sins and adoption into the family of God. But the truth is that the Holy Spirit witnesses to much more than this.

He witnesses to sinful souls that they are guilty, condemned before God, and lost. This we call conviction, but it is none other than the witness of the Spirit to our true condition. And when we realize it, nothing can convince us to the contrary. Our friends may point out our good works, our kindly disposition, and try to assure us that we are not a bad person. But so long as the Spirit continues to witness to our guilt, nothing can console us or reassure our quaking heart. This convicting witness may come at any time, but it is usually given under the searching preaching of the gospel or by the burning testimony of those who have been gloriously saved and sanctified, or in time of danger, when the soul is awed into silence so that it can hear the "still small voice" of the Holy Spirit.

The Holy Spirit also witnesses not only to the forgiveness of sins and acceptance with God, but also to sanctification. "For by a single offering," said the author of Hebrews, "he has perfected for all time those who are being sanctified. And the Holy Spirit also bears witness to us" (Heb. 10:14–15 ESV).

Indeed, one who has this witness can no more doubt it than someone with two good eyes can doubt the existence of the sun when stepping forth into the splendor of a cloudless noonday. It satisfies and prompts the exulting cry, "We know, we know!"

Paul seemed to teach that the Holy Spirit witnesses to every good thing God works in us, for he said, "We have received, not the spirit of the world, but the spirit which is of God; that we might know the things that are freely given to us of God" (1 Cor. 2:12 KJV). It is for our comfort and encouragement to know our acceptance of God and our rights, privileges, and possessions in Jesus Christ, and the Holy Spirit is given for this purpose—that we may know.

But it is important to bear in mind God's plan of work in this matter.

The witness of the Spirit is dependent upon our faith. God does not give it to those who do not believe in Jesus. And if our faith wavers, the witness will become intermittent. If faith fails, it will be withdrawn. Owing to the unsteadiness of their faith, many new Christians get into uncertainty. Happy are they at such times if someone is at hand to instruct and encourage them to look steadfastly to Jesus. Unfortunately, many Christians of longer experience, through unsteady faith, walk in gloom and uncertainty and, instead of encouraging newer believers, they discourage them. Steadfast faith will keep the inward witness bright.

We must not get our attention off Jesus, and the promises of God in Him, and fix it upon the witness of the Spirit. The witness continues only while we look to Jesus and trust and obey Him. When we take our eyes off Him, the witness is gone. Many people fail here. Instead of quietly and confidently looking to Jesus and trusting Him, they vainly look for the witness—which is like trying to realize the sweetness of honey without receiving it in your mouth, or the beauty of a picture while looking inward upon oneself instead of outward upon the picture. Jesus saves. Look to Him, and He will send the Spirit to witness to His work.

The witness may be brightened by diligence in the discharge of duty, frequent seasons of glad prayer, definite testimony to salvation and sanctification, and by stirring up our faith.

The witness may be dulled by neglect of duty, sloth in prayer, inattention to the Bible, indefinite and hesitating testimony, and by carelessness, when we should be careful to walk soberly and steadfastly with the Lord.

I dare not say that the witness of the Spirit is dependent upon our health, but there are some forms of nervous and organic disease that seem to so distract or becloud the mind as to interfere with the clear discernment of the witness of the Spirit. I knew a nervous little child who when being carried across the street in her father's arms would be so distracted with fear by an approaching carriage that she seemed to be incapable of hearing or heeding his reassuring voice. It may be that there are some diseases that for the time prevent the sufferer from discerning the reassuring witness of the heavenly Father. Dr. Asa Mahan told me of an experience of this kind which he had during a very dangerous sickness. And Dr. Daniel Steele had a similar experience while lying at the point of death with typhoid fever. But some of the happiest Christians the world has seen have been racked with pain and tortured with disease. And so, while there may be seasons of fierce temptation when the witness is not clearly discerned, we may rest assured that if our hearts cleave to Jesus Christ and duty, He will never leave or forsake us.

But the witness will be lost if we willfully sin or persistently neglect to follow where He leads. This witness is a pearl of great price, and Satan will try to steal it from us. Therefore, we must continually guard it with watchful prayer.

If lost, the witness may be found again by prayer and faith and a dutiful taking up of the cross that has been laid down. Thousands who have lost it have found it again, and often they have found it with increased brightness and glory. If you have lost it, look up in faith to your loving God, and He will restore it to you. It is possible to live on the right side of plain duty without the witness, but you cannot be sure of your salvation, joyful in service, or glad in God, without it. And since it is promised to all God's children, no one who professes to be His should be without it.

If you do not have it, seek it now by faith in Jesus. Go to Him, and do not let Him go till He notifies you that you are His. Listen to Charles Wesley:

> From the world of sin, and noise,
> And hurry, I withdraw;
> For the small and inward voice
> I wait with humble awe;
> Silent am I now and still,
> Dare not in Thy presence move;
> To my waiting soul reveal
> The secret of Thy love.[6]

Do you want the witness to abide? Then study the Word of God and live by it. Sing and make melody in your heart to the Lord. Praise the Lord with your first waking breath in the morning, and thank Him with your last waking breath at night. Flee from sin. Keep on believing. Look to Jesus, cleave to Him, follow Him gladly, trust the efficacy of His blood, and the witness will abide in your heart. Be patient with the Lord. Let Him mold you, and "He will take delight in you with gladness. With his love, he will calm all your fears. He will rejoice over you with joyful songs" (Zeph. 3:17 NLT), and you shall no longer doubt, but know that you are His.

There are in this loud stunning tide
Of human care and crime,
With whom the melodies abide
Of th' everlasting chime;
Who carry music in their heart
Through dusky lane and wrangling mart,
Plying their task with busier feet
Because their secret souls a holy strain repeat.[7]

And that "holy strain" is but the echo of the Lord's song in their hearts, which is the witness of the Spirit.

NOTES

1. Philip Doddridge, "Sovereign of All the Worlds on High," 1739, public domain.

2. Source unknown.

3. John Wesley, *Sermons on Several Occasions* (Hudson: William E. Norman, 1810), 311.

4. Charles Wesley, "Arise, My Soul, Arise," 1742, public domain.

5. Charles Wesley, "How Can a Sinner Know His Sins on Earth Forgiven?," 1749, public domain.

6. Charles Wesley, "Open, Lord, My Inward Ear," 1812, public domain.

7. John Keble, "There Are in This Loud Stunning Tide," *Old Favourites from the Elder Poets with a Few Newer Friends*, ed. Matilda Sharpe (London: Williams and Norgate, 1881), 338.

Purity

A minister of the gospel, after listening to an eminent servant of God preaching on entire sanctification through the baptism with the Spirit, wrote to him, saying, "I like your teaching on the baptism with the Holy Ghost. I need it, and am seeking it; but I do not care much for entire sanctification or heart cleansing. Pray for me that I may be filled with the Holy Ghost."

The brother knew him well, and immediately replied, "I am so glad you believe in the baptism with the Holy Ghost and are so earnestly seeking it. I join my prayer with yours that you may receive that gift. But let me say to you, that if you get the gift of the Holy Ghost, you will have to take entire sanctification with it, for the first thing the baptism with the Holy Ghost does is to cleanse the heart from all sin." Thank God, he humbled himself and permitted the Lord to sanctify him. And he was filled with the Holy Spirit and mightily empowered to work for God.

Many have looked at the promise of power when the Holy Spirit is come, the energy of Peter's preaching on the day of Pentecost, and the marvelous results which followed, and have hastily and erroneously jumped to the conclusion that the baptism with the Holy Spirit is for work and service only.

It does bring power—the power of God. And it does fit for service, probably the most important service to which any created beings are commissioned—the proclamation of salvation and the conditions of peace to a lost world. But not that alone, nor primarily. The primary, the basal work of the baptism, is that of cleansing.

You may turn a flood into your millrun, but until it sweeps away the logs and brushwood and dirt that obstruct the course, you cannot get power to turn the wheels of your mill. The flood first washes out the obstructions, and then you have power.

The great hindrance in the hearts of God's children to the Holy Spirit's power is inbred sin—that dark, defiant, evil something within that struggles for the mastery of the soul and will not submit to be meek and lowly and patient and forbearing and holy, as was Jesus. And when the Holy Spirit comes, His first work is to sweep away that something, that carnal principle, and make free and clean all the channels of the soul.

Peter was filled with power on the day of Pentecost. But evidently the baptism's purifying effect made a deeper and more lasting impression upon his mind than the empowering effect, for years after, in the Council of Jerusalem, he stood up and told about the spiritual baptism of Cornelius, the Roman centurion, and his household. He said, "God, who knows the heart, acknowledged them by giving them the Holy Spirit, just as He did to us, and made no distinction between us and them, purifying their hearts by faith" (Acts 15:8–9 NKJV). He called attention not to power, but to purity, as the baptism's effect. When the Holy Spirit comes in to abide, the old, sinful nature goes out.

This destruction of inbred sin is made perfectly plain in that wonderful Old Testament type of the baptism with the Holy Spirit and fire recorded in the sixth chapter of Isaiah. The prophet was a most earnest preacher of righteousness (see Isa. 1:10–20), yet he was not sanctified wholly. But he had a vision of the Lord upon His throne and of the seraphim crying one to another, "Holy, holy, holy is the LORD of Heaven's Armies! The whole earth is filled with his glory!" (Isa. 6:3 NLT). "Their voices shook the Temple to its foundations"—and how much more should the heart of the prophet be moved! And so it was. He cried out, "It's all over! I am doomed, for I am a sinful man. I have filthy lips, and I live among a people with filthy lips. Yet I have seen the King, the LORD of Heaven's Armies" (Isa. 6:4–5 NLT).

When unsanctified people have a vision of God, it is not their lack of power that troubles them, but their lack of purity, their unlikeness to Christ, the Holy One. And so it was with the prophet. But he added, "Then one of the seraphim flew to me with a burning coal he had taken from the altar with a pair of tongs. He touched my lips with it and said, 'See, this coal has touched your lips. Now your guilt is removed, and your sins are forgiven'" (Isa. 6:6–7 NLT). Again, it is purity rather than power to which our attention is directed.

We have another type of this spiritual baptism in the thirty-sixth chapter of Ezekiel. In Isaiah the type was that of fire, but in Ezekiel it is that of water—for water and oil, and the wind and rain and dew, are all used as types of the Holy Spirit.

The Lord said through Ezekiel, "Then I will sprinkle clean water on you, and you will be clean. Your filth will be washed away, and you will no longer worship idols. And I will give you a new heart, and I will put a new spirit in you. I will take out your stony, stubborn heart and give you a tender, responsive heart. And I will put my Spirit in you so that you will follow my decrees and be careful to obey my regulations" (Ezek. 36:25–27 NLT).

Once again, the incoming of the Holy Spirit means the outgoing of all sin, of all "your filth . . . and you will no longer worship idols." How plainly it is taught! Yet many of God's dear children do not believe it is their privilege to be free from sin and pure in heart in this life. But, may we not? Let us consider this.

It is certainly desirable. Every sincere Christian—and none can be a Christian who is not sincere—wants to be free from sin, to be pure in heart, to be like Christ. Sin is hateful to every true child of God. The Spirit within us cries out against the sin, the wrong temper, the pride, the lust, the selfishness, the evil that lurks within the heart. Surely, it is desirable to be free from sin.

He wills that I should holy be:

That holiness I long to feel;

That full Divine conformity

To all my Savior's righteous will.[1]

It is necessary, for "those who are not holy will not see the Lord" (Heb. 12:14 NLT). Sometime, somehow, somewhere, sin must go out of our hearts—all sin—or we cannot go into heaven. Sin would spoil heaven just as it spoils earth, just as it spoils the peace of hearts and homes, of families and neighborhoods and nations here. Why God in His wisdom allows sin in the world, I do not know, I cannot understand. But this I understand: that He has one world into which He will not let sin enter. He has notified us in advance that no sin— nothing that defiles—can enter heaven and mar the blessedness of that holy place. "Who may climb the mountain of the LORD? Who may stand in his holy place? Only those whose hands and hearts are pure, who do not worship idols and never tell lies" (Ps. 24:3–4 NLT). We must get rid of sin to get into heaven, to enjoy the full favor of God. It is necessary.

> Choose I must, and soon must choose
> Holiness, or heaven lose.
> If what heaven loves I hate,
> Shut for me is heaven's gate!

> Endless sin means endless woe;
> Into endless sin I go
> If my soul, from reason rent,
> Takes from sin its final bent.

> As the stream its channel grooves,
> And within that channel moves;
> So does habit's deepest tide
> Groove its bed and there abide.

Light obeyed increaseth light;

Light resisted bringeth night;

Who shall give me will to choose

If the love of light I lose?

Speed, my soul, this instant yield;

Let the light its scepter wield.

While thy God prolongs His grace,

Haste thee to His holy face.[2]

This purification from sin is promised. Nothing can be plainer than God's promise on this point. "Then I will sprinkle clean water on you, and you will be clean. Your filth will be washed away, and you will no longer worship idols" (Ezek. 36:25 NLT). When all is removed, nothing remains. When all filthiness and all idols are taken away, none are left.

"Where sin abounded, grace abounded much more, so that as sin reigned in death, even so grace might reign through righteousness to eternal life through Jesus Christ our Lord" (Rom. 5:20–21 NKJV). Grace reigns, not through sin, but "through righteousness" which has expelled sin. Grace brings in righteousness and sin goes out: "If we are living in the light, as God is in the light, then we have fellowship with each other, and the blood of Jesus, his Son, cleanses us from all sin" (1 John 1:7 NLT). "Having been set free from sin, you became slaves of righteousness" (Rom. 6:18 NKJV).

These are sample promises and assurances, any one of which is sufficient to encourage us to believe that our heavenly Father will save us from all sin, if we meet His conditions.

This deliverance is possible. It was for this that Jesus Christ, the Father's Son, came into the world and suffered and died, that He might "save his people from their sins" (Matt. 1:21 KJV). It was for this that He shed His precious blood—to cleanse us from all sin. It was for this that the Word of God, with its wonderful promises, was given, that we may "share his divine nature and escape the world's corruption caused by human desires" (2 Pet. 1:4 NLT), by which is meant escape from inbred sin. It was for this that ministers of the gospel are given to the church "for the perfecting of the saints" (Eph. 4:12 KJV) and for the saving and sanctifying of souls (see Acts 26:18). It is primarily for this that the Holy Spirit comes as a baptism of fire—that sin might be consumed out of us, so that we might "share in the inheritance that belongs to his people, who live in the light" (Col. 1:12 NLT), that we might be ready without a moment's warning to go into the midst of the heavenly hosts in white garments, washed in the blood of the Lamb.

And shall all these mighty agents and this heavenly provision and these gracious purposes of God fail to destroy sin out of any obedient, believing heart? Is sin omnipotent? No!

If you will look to Jesus right now, trusting the merits of His blood, and receive the Holy Spirit into your heart, you shall be "made free from sin" (Rom. 6:18 KJV). It "shall not have dominion over you" (Rom. 6:14 KJV). Under the fiery touch of His holy presence, your iniquity shall be taken away and your sin shall be purged. And you yourself shall burn like the bush Moses saw—yet, like the bush, you shall not be consumed. And by this holy fire, this flame of love that consumes sin, you shall be made proof against that unquenchable fire that consumes sinners.

Come, Holy Ghost, Thy mighty aid bestowing;

Destroy the works of sin, the self, the pride;

Burn, burn in me, my idols overthrowing:

Prepare my heart for Him, for my Lord crucified.[3]

NOTES

1. Charles Wesley, "He Wills That I Should Holy Be," 1762, public domain.

2. Joseph Cook, "God's Time Now," 1887, public domain.

3. Catherine Booth-Clibborn, "At Thy Feet I Fall," *The Salvation Army Songbook*, 1884, public domain.

Power  6

Just before His ascension, Jesus met His disciples for the last time, repeated His command, "Do not leave Jerusalem until the Father sends you the gift he promised," and reiterated His promise that they would soon be "be baptized with the Holy Spirit" (Acts 1:4–5 NLT).

Then they asked Him, "Lord, has the time come for you to free Israel and restore our kingdom?" They were still eager for an earthly kingdom. But He said, "The Father alone has the authority to set those dates and times, and they are not for you to know." And then He added, "But you will receive power when the Holy Spirit comes upon you" (Acts 1:6 NLT).

They wanted power and He assured them they would have it, but said nothing of its nature or of the work and activities into which it would thrust them and for which it would equip them, beyond the fact that they would be His witnesses, "telling people about me everywhere — in

Jerusalem, throughout Judea, in Samaria, and to the ends of the earth"
(Acts 1:8 NLT). After that, the Holy Spirit Himself was to be their
teacher.

And then Jesus left them. Earth lost its power to hold Him, and
while they beheld Him, He began to ascend — a cloud bent low from
heaven, receiving Him out of sight, and they were left alone, with His
promise of power ringing in their ears and His command to wait for
the promise of the Father checking any impatience that might lead
them to go fishing (as Peter had done some days before), or cause an
undue haste to begin their life work of witnessing for Him before
God's appointed time.

For ten days they waited, not listlessly, but eagerly, as a maid for
her mistress or a servant for a master who is expected to come at any
moment. They forgot their personal ambitions. They ceased to judge
and criticize one another, and in the sweet unity of brotherly love, "with
one accord" (Acts 2:1 KJV) they rejoiced, prayed, and waited. And then
on the day of Pentecost, at their early morning prayer meeting, when
they were all present, the windows of heaven opened, and such a blessing as they could not contain was poured out upon them: "Suddenly,
there was a sound from heaven like the roaring of a mighty windstorm,
and it filled the house where they were sitting. Then, what looked like
flames or tongues of fire appeared and settled on each of them. And
everyone present was filled with the Holy Spirit" (Acts 2:2–4 NLT). This
was the inaugural day of the church of God, the dawn of the dispen-
sation of the Holy Spirit, the beginning of the days of power.

In the morning of that day, there were only a few Christians in the
world. The New Testament was not written, and it is doubtful if they

had among them all a copy of the Old Testament. They had no church buildings, colleges, or religious books and papers. They were poor and despised, unlearned and ignorant. But before night they had enrolled three thousand new followers from among those who a few weeks before had crucified their Lord, and they had aroused and filled all Jerusalem with questionings and amazement. What was the secret? Power. What was the source? God the Holy Spirit. He had come, and this work was His work. And they were His instruments.

When Jesus came, a body was prepared for Him (see Heb. 10:5) and through that body He performed His wondrous works. But when the other Comforter comes, He takes possession of those bodies that are freely and fully presented to Him, and He touches their lips with grace. He shines peacefully and gloriously on their faces. He flashes beams of pity, compassion, and heavenly affection from their eyes. He kindles a fire of love in their hearts and lights the flame of truth in their minds. They become His temple, and their hearts are a Holy of Holies in which His blessed presence ever abides. And from that central citadel He works, enduing all who have received Him with power.

If you ask how the Holy Spirit can dwell within us and work through us without destroying our personality, I cannot tell. How can electricity fill and transform a dead wire into a live one, which you dare not touch? How can a magnetic current fill a piece of steel and transform it into a mighty force which by its touch can raise tons of iron as a child would lift a feather? How can fire dwell in a piece of iron until its very appearance is that of fire and it becomes a firebrand? I cannot tell.

Now, what fire and electricity and magnetism do in iron and steel, the Holy Spirit does in the spirits of those who believe in Jesus, follow

Him wholly, and trust Him intelligently. He dwells in them and inspires them, till they are all alive with the very life of God.

The transformation wrought in us by the baptism with the Holy Spirit, and the power that fills us, are amazing beyond measure. The Holy Spirit gives power.

1. Power over the world. They become "dead to the world and all its toys, its idle pomps and fading joys."[1] The world masters and enslaves people who do not have the Holy Spirit. To one it offers money, and he falls down and worships, selling his conscience and character for gold. To another it offers power, and she falls down and worships and sacrifices her principles and sears her conscience for power. To another it offers pleasure, to another learning, to another fame, and they fall down and worship and sell themselves for these things. But men and women who are filled with the Holy Spirit are free. They can turn from these things without a pang, as they would from pebbles. Or they can take them and use them as their servants for the glory of God and the good of others.

What did Peter and James and John care for the great places in the kingdoms of this world after they were filled with the Holy Spirit? They would not have exchanged places with Herod the king or with Caesar himself. For the gratification of any personal ambition these things were no more attractive to them now than the lordship over a tribe of ants on their tiny hill. They were now kings and priests unto God. Theirs was an everlasting kingdom, and its glory exceeds the glory of the kingdoms of this world as the splendor of the sun exceeds that of the glowworm.

The head of some great business enterprises was making many thousands of dollars every year, but when the Holy Spirit filled him, money lost its power over him. He still retained his position and made vast sums. But as a steward of the Lord, he poured it into God's work, and has been doing so for more than thirty years.

The disciples in Jerusalem after Pentecost held all their possessions in common, so completely were they freed from the power and love of money.

A rising young lawyer was filled with the Spirit and the next day said to his client, "I cannot plead your case. I have a retainer from the Lord Jesus." And he became one of the mightiest preachers the world has ever seen.

A popular boy got the fiery baptism and went to his baseball team and said, "Boys, you swear, and I am now a Christian and cannot play with you anymore." And God made him the wonder of all his old friends and a happy winner of souls.

A fashionable woman got the baptism, and God gave her power to break away from her worldly set and surroundings and to live wholly for Him. And He gave her an influence that circled the globe.

Paul said, "The world is crucified unto me, and I unto the world" (Gal. 6:14 KJV). Men could whip and stone and imprison his body and cut off his head, but his soul was free. It was enslaved and driven by no unholy or inordinate ambition, no lust for gold, no desire for power or fame, no fear of others, no shame of worldly censure or adverse public opinion. He had power over the world, and this same power is the birthright of every follower of Jesus, and the present possession of everyone who is wholly sanctified by the baptism with the Holy Spirit.

2. Power over the flesh. The body, which God intended for a "house beautiful" for the soul and a temple holy unto Himself, is often

reduced to a sty, where the imprisoned soul wallows in lusts and passions, and degrades itself below the level of beasts. But this baptism gives a person power over his or her body.

God has given us such desires and passions as are necessary to secure our continued existence, and not one is in itself evil, but good and only good. And these, when controlled and used—but not abused—will help to develop and maintain the purest and highest humanity. The appetites for food and drink are necessary to life. Another desire is intended to secure the continuance of the human race. And so all the desires and appetites of the body have useful ends, were given to us in love by our heavenly Father for high and essential purposes, and are necessary to us as human beings.

The soul that is cut off by sin from fellowship with God, however, seeks satisfaction in sensual excesses and in the unlawful gratification of these appetites, and so sinks to depths of degradation to which no beast ever falls. That soul then becomes a slave, as swollen and raging passion takes the place of innocent appetites and desires.

But when the Holy Spirit enters the heart and sanctifies the soul, He does not destroy these desires but purifies and regulates them. He reinforces the soul with the fear and love of God, and gives it power, complete power, over the fleshly appetites. He restores it to its full fellowship with God and its kingship over the body.

While these appetites and desires are not in themselves sinful, but are necessary for our welfare and our complete humanity, and while their diseased and abnormal power is cured when we are sanctified, they are still avenues through which we may be tempted. Therefore, they must be guarded with care and ruled in wisdom.

Many people stumble at and reject the doctrine of entire sanctification because they do not understand these things. They mistake that which is natural and essential to a human being for the diseased and abnormal propensity caused by sin, and so miss the blessed truth of full salvation.

I knew a doctor who had used tobacco for over sixty years, who was delivered from the abnormal appetite instantly through the sanctification of the Spirit. I knew an old man who had been a drunkard for over fifty years, similarly delivered. I knew a young man, the slave of a vicious habit of the flesh, who was set free at once by the fiery baptism. Electrical current cannot transform the dead wire into a live one quicker than the Holy Spirit can flood a soul with light and love, destroy the carnal mind, and fill a soul with power over all sin.

3. Power over the Devil. The indwelling presence of the Holy Spirit destroys all doubt as to the personality of the Devil. He is discerned, and his malice is felt and known as never before.

A soldier may be so skillfully attacked in the dark that the enemy is not discovered—but not in the day. Many people in these days deny that there is any Devil, only evil. But they are in the dark, so much in the dark that they not only say that there is no Devil, but that there is no personal God, only good. But the day comes with the Holy Spirit's entrance, and then God is intimately known and the Devil is discovered. And as he assailed Jesus after His baptism with the Spirit, so he does today all who receive the Holy Spirit. He comes as an angel of light to deceive, and as a roaring lion to devour and overcome with fear. But the soul filled with the Spirit outwits the Devil and, clad in the whole armor of God, overcomes the old Enemy.

"Power . . . over all the power of the enemy" (Luke 10:19 KJV) is God's purpose for all His children. Power to do the will of God patiently and effectively, with naturalness and ease, or to suffer the will of God with patience and good cheer, comes with this blessed baptism. It is power for service or sacrifice, according to God's will. Have you this power? If not, it is for you. Yield yourself fully to Christ right now, and if you ask in faith you shall receive.

NOTE

1. Charles Wesley, "Come, Jesus, Lord, with Holy Fire," 1880, public domain.

Testing the Spirits 7

Those who do not have the Holy Spirit, or who do not heed Him, fall easily and naturally into formalism, substituting lifeless ceremonies, sacraments, genuflections, and ritualistic performances for the free, glad, living worship inspired by the indwelling Spirit. They sing, but not from the heart. They say their prayers, but they do not really pray.

"I prayed last night, Mother," said a child.

"Why, my child, you pray every night!" replied the mother.

"No," said the child, "I only said prayers, but last night I really prayed." And his face shone. He had opened his heart to the Holy Spirit and had at last really talked with God and worshiped.

But those who receive the Holy Spirit may fall into fanaticism, unless they follow the command of John to "test the spirits to see whether they are from God" (1 John 4:1 NIV).

We are commanded not to "scoff at prophecies," but at the same time we are told to "test everything" (1 Thess. 5:20–21 NLT). "There are many false prophets in the world" (1 John 4:1 NLT) and they will lead us astray, if possible. So we must beware. As someone has written, we must "believe not every spirit; regard not, trust not, follow not every pretender to the Spirit of God, or every professor of vision, or inspiration, or revelation from God."[1]

The higher and more intense the life, the more carefully must it be guarded, lest it be endangered and go astray. It is so in the natural world and likewise in the spiritual world.

When Satan can no longer rock people to sleep with religious lullabies or satisfy them with the lifeless form, then he comes as an angel of light, probably in the person of some purveyor or teacher of religion, and seeks to usurp the place of the Holy Spirit. But instead of leading "into all truth," he leads the unwary soul into deadly error. Instead of directing people onto the highway of holiness and into the path of perfect peace, where no ravenous beast ever comes, he leads them into a wilderness where their souls, stripped of the beautiful garments of salvation, are robbed and wounded and left to die, unless some Good Samaritan, with patient pity and Christlike love, comes that way.

When the Holy Spirit comes in His fullness, He strips us of our self-righteousness and pride and conceit. We see ourselves as the chief of sinners and realize that only through Jesus' stripes are we healed, and ever after, as we live in the Spirit, our boast is in Him and our glory is in the cross. Remembering the hole of the pit from which we were quarried, we are filled with tender pity for all who are not in the

Way. And, while we do not excuse or belittle sin, yet we are slow to
believe evil and our judgments are full of charity.

> Judge not; the workings of his brain
> And of his heart thou canst not see:
> What looks to thy dim eyes a stain,
> In God's pure light may only be
> A scar, brought from some well-won field,
> Where thou wouldst only faint and yield.[2]

But people who have been thus snared by Satan forget their own
past miserable state, boast of their righteousness, thank God that they
are not like others, and begin to beat their fellow servants with heavy
denunciations, thrust them through with sharp criticisms, and pelt
them with hard words. They cease to pity and begin to condemn. They
no longer warn and entreat others in tender love but are quick to
believe evil and swift to pass judgment not only upon others' actions,
but upon their motives as well.

True charity does not wink at iniquity, but it is as far removed from
a sharp, condemning spirit as light is from darkness and as honey is
from vinegar. It is quick to condemn sin, but is full of saving, long-
suffering compassion for the sinner.

A humble, teachable mind marks those in whom the Holy Spirit
dwells. They esteem very highly in love those who are over them in
the Lord and are glad to be admonished by them. They submit themselves one to the other, welcome instruction and correction, and
esteem "open rebuke . . . better than secret love" (Prov. 27:5 KJV).

They believe that the Lord has yet many things to say to them, and they are willing and glad for Him to say them by whomever He will, but especially by their leaders and their brothers and sisters. While they do not fawn and cringe before others or believe everything that is said to them without proving it by the Word and Spirit of God, they believe that God "gave some to be apostles, some prophets, some evangelists, and some pastors and teachers, for the equipping of the saints for the work of ministry, for the edifying of the body of Christ" (Eph. 4:11–12 NKJV) and, like Cornelius, they are ready to hear these appointed ministers and receive the word of the Lord from them.

But Satan seeks to destroy all this lowliness of spirit and humbleness of mind. Those in whom his deadly work has begun are wiser in their own conceit "than seven [people] who can answer sensibly" (Prov. 26:16 ESV). They are wiser than all their teachers, and no one can instruct them. One of these deluded souls, who had previously been marked by modesty and humility, declared of certain of God's chosen leaders whose spiritual knowledge and wisdom were everywhere recognized, that "the whole of them knew no more about the Holy Ghost than an old goose." Paul, Luther, and Wesley were much troubled, and their work greatly hurt, by some of these misguided souls, and every great spiritual awakening is likely to be marred more or less by such people, so that we cannot be too much on our guard against false spirits who would counterfeit the work and leadings of the Holy Spirit.

It is this huge conceit that has led some to announce themselves as apostles and prophets to whom all must listen or fall under God's wrath, while others have declared that they were living in resurrection bodies and should not die. Still others have reached that pitch of fanaticism where they could calmly proclaim themselves to be the Messiah or the Holy Spirit in bodily form. Such people will be quick to deny the infallibility of the pope, while they assume their own infallibility and denounce all who dispute it.

The Holy Spirit may lead to a holy rivalry in love and humility, and kindness and self-denial and good works, but He never leads His servants into such swelling conceit that they can no longer be taught by others.

Those who are filled with the Spirit are tolerant of others who may differ from them in opinion or in doctrine. They are firm in their own convictions, and ready at all times with meekness and fear to explain and defend the doctrines which they hold and are convinced are according to God's Word, but they do not condemn all those who differ. They are glad to believe that people are often better than their creed and may be saved in spite of it. Like mountains whose bases are bathed with sunshine and clothed with fruitful fields and vineyards while their tops are covered with dark clouds, so human hearts are often fruitful in the graces of charity while their heads are yet darkened by doctrinal error.

Anyway, as servants of the Lord, they will "not be quarrelsome but kind to everyone, able to teach, patiently enduring evil, correcting . . . opponents with gentleness. [For] God may perhaps grant them repentance leading to a knowledge of the truth, and they may come to their senses and escape from the snare of the devil, after being captured by him to do his will" (2 Tim. 2:24–26 ESV).

But Satan, under guise of love for and loyalty to the truth, will introduce the spirit of intolerance. It was this spirit that crucified Jesus, burned John Hus at the stake, hanged Girolamo Savonarola, and inspired the massacre of St. Bartholomew and the horrors of the Inquisition. And the same spirit (in a milder but possibly more subtle form) blinds the eyes of many professing Christians to any good in those who differ from them in doctrine, forms of worship, or methods of government. They murder love to protect what they often blindly call truth. What is truth without love? A dead thing, an encumbrance, "the letter [that] kills" (2 Cor. 3:6 ESV).

The body is necessary to our life in this world, but life can exist in a deformed and even mutilated body. And such a body with life in it is better than the most perfect body that is only a corpse. So, while truth is most precious, and sound doctrine to be esteemed more than silver and gold, yet love can exist where truth is not held in its most perfect and complete forms, and love is the one thing needful.

> The love of God is broader
> Than the measure of man's mind:
> And the heart of the Eternal
> Is most wonderfully kind.[3]

The Holy Spirit produces a spirit of unity among Christians. People who have been sitting behind their sectarian fences in self-complacent ease, proselytizing zeal, or grim defiance are suddenly lifted above the fence and find sweet fellowship with each other when He comes into their hearts.

They delight in each other's company. They esteem others better than themselves, and in honor they prefer one another before themselves (see Phil. 2:3; Rom. 12:10). They fulfill the psalmist's ideal: "How good and pleasant it is when God's people live together in unity!"

(Ps. 133:1 NIV). Here is a picture of the unity of Christians in the beginning in Jerusalem: "And they were all filled with the Holy Spirit. Then they preached the word of God with boldness. All the believers were united in heart and mind. And they felt that what they owned was not their own, so they shared everything they had" (Acts 4:31–32 NLT).

What an ideal this is! And since it has been attained once, it can be attained again and retained, but only by the indwelling of the Holy Spirit. It was for this that Jesus poured out His heart in His great intercessory prayer just before His arrest in the garden of Gethsemane: "I am praying not only for these disciples but also for all who will ever believe in me through their message. I pray that they will all be one" (John 17:20–21 NLT). And what was the standard of unity to which He would have us come? Listen: "As you are in me, Father, and I am in you. And may they be in us so that the world will believe you sent me" (John 17:21 NLT). Such unity has a wondrous power to compel the belief of worldly men and women. "I have given them the glory you gave me, so they may be one as we are one. I am in them and you are in me. May they experience such perfect unity that the world will know that you sent me and that you love them as much as you love me" (John 17:22–23 NLT). Wondrous unity! Wondrous love!

It is for this His blessed heart eternally yearns, and it is for this that the Holy Spirit works in the hearts of those who receive Him. But Satan constantly seeks to destroy this holy love and divine unity. When he comes, he arouses suspicions, stirs up strife, quenches the spirit of intercessory prayer, engenders backbiting, and causes separations.

After enumerating various Christian graces, and urging the Colossians to put them on, Paul wrote, "Above all, clothe yourselves with love, which binds us all together in perfect harmony" (Col. 3:14 NLT). These graces were garments, and love was the belt that bound and held them together—and so love is the bond that holds true Christians together.

Divine love is the great test by which we are to measure ourselves and all teachers and spirits.

Love is not puffed up. Love is not bigoted. Love is not intolerant. Love is not schismatic. Love is loyal to Jesus and to all His people. If we have this love shed abroad in our hearts by the Holy Spirit (see Rom. 5:5), we shall discern the voice of our Good Shepherd and shall not be deceived by the voice of the stranger. And so we shall be saved from both formalism and fanaticism.

NOTES

1. Matthew Henry, *An Exposition of All the Books of the Old and New Testaments*, vol. 5 (London: W. Baynes, 1806), 639.

2. Adelaide A. Procter, "Judge Not," n. d., public domain.

3. Frederick W. Faber, "There's a Wideness in God's Mercy," 1854, public domain.

Guidance

It is the work of the Holy Spirit to guide God's people through the uncertainties and dangers and duties of this life to their home in heaven. When He led the children of Israel out of Egypt by the hand of Moses, He guided them through the mountainous wilderness in a pillar of cloud by day and of fire by night, thus assuring their comfort and safety. And this was but a type of His perpetual spiritual guidance of His people.

"But how may I know for certain what God wants of me?" is sure to be the earnest and, often, agonizing cry of every humble and devoutly zealous young Christian. "How may I know the guidance of the Holy Spirit?"

We must get it fixed in our minds that we need to be guided always by Him. A ship was wrecked on a rocky coast far off the course that the captain thought he was taking. On examination, it was found that the compass had been slightly deflected by a bit of metal that had lodged in the box.

The voyage of life on which we sail is beset by as many dangers as the ship at sea, and how shall we surely steer our course to our heavenly harbor without divine guidance? There is a nearly infinite number of influences to deflect us from the safe and certain course. We start out in the morning and we know not what person we may meet, what paragraph we may read, what word may be spoken, what letter we may receive, what subtle temptation may assail or allure us, or what immediate decisions we may have to make during the day, that may turn us almost imperceptibly but nonetheless surely from the right way. We need the guidance of the Holy Spirit.

We not only need divine guidance, but we may have it. God's Word assures us of this: "The LORD will guide you continually" (Isa. 58:11 ESV). Not occasionally, not spasmodically, but "continually." The psalmist said, "This is God, our God forever and ever. He will guide us forever" (Ps. 48:14 ESV). Jesus said of the Holy Spirit, "When the Spirit of truth comes, he will guide you into all truth" (John 16:13 NLT). And Paul wrote, "All who are led by the Spirit of God are children of God" (Rom. 8:14 NLT).

These Scriptures establish the fact that the children of God may be guided always by the Spirit of God.

> Guide me, O Thou great Jehovah,
> Pilgrim through this barren land!
> I am weak, but Thou art mighty:
> Hold me with Thy powerful hand.[1]

How does God guide us? "The LORD says, 'I will guide you along the best pathway for your life'" (Ps. 32:8 NLT). He does this in a number of ways:

- By faith. Paul said, "We walk by faith, not by sight" (2 Cor. 5:7 KJV) and, "The just shall live by faith" (Rom. 1:17 KJV). So we may conclude that God never leads us in such a way as to do away with the necessity of faith. We read that when God warned Noah, it was by faith that Noah was led to build the ark (see Heb. 11:7). When God told Abraham to go to a land which He would show him, it was by faith that Abraham went (see Heb. 11: 8). If we believe, we will surely be guided. But if we do not believe, we shall be left to ourselves. Without faith it is impossible to please God or to follow where He leads.
- By "sanctified common sense." The Spirit guides us in such manner as to demand the exercise of our best judgment. He enlightens our understanding and directs our judgment by sound reason and sense. As the psalmist said, "The meek will he guide in judgment" (Ps. 25:9 KJV).

I knew a man who was eager to obey God and be led by the Spirit but had the mistaken idea that the Holy Spirit sets aside human judgment and common sense and speaks directly upon the minutest and most commonplace matters. He wanted the Holy Spirit to direct him just how much to eat at each meal, and he has been known to take food out of his mouth at what he supposed to be the Holy Spirit's notification that he had eaten enough. He believed that if he swallowed that mouthful, it would be in violation of the leadings of the Spirit.

No doubt, the Spirit will help an honest person to arrive at a safe judgment even in matters of this kind, but it will be through the use of sanctified common sense. Otherwise, we would be reduced to a state of mental infancy and kept in intellectual swaddling clothes. He will guide us, but only as we resolutely — and in the best light we have — exercise judgment. John Wesley said that God usually guided him by presenting reasons to his mind for any given course of action.

• By enlightening our study. The psalmist received a promise: "The LORD says . . . 'I will advise you and watch over you'" (Ps. 32:8 NLT). And the psalmist affirmed this had proven true when he said, "You guide me with your counsel, leading me to a glorious destiny" (Ps. 73:24 NLT). Now, advice, counsel, instruction, and teaching not only imply effort upon the part of the teacher, but also study and close attention on the part of the one being taught. The guidance of the Holy Spirit will require us to listen attentively, study diligently, and patiently learn the lessons He would teach us. The Holy Spirit does not set aside our powers and faculties but seeks to awaken and stir them into full activity and develop them into well-rounded perfection, thus making them channels through which He can intelligently influence and direct us. He seeks to illuminate our whole spiritual being as the sun illuminates our physical being, and to bring us into such union and sympathy, such oneness of thought, desire, affection, and purpose with God, that we shall know at all times, by a kind of spiritual instinct, the mind of God concerning us, and never be in doubt about His will.

- By opening up to our minds the deep, sanctifying truths of the Bible, especially by revealing to us the character and spirit of Jesus and His apostles, and leading us to follow in their footsteps—the footsteps of their faith and love and unselfish devotion to God and others, even to the laying down of their lives.
- By the circumstances and surroundings of our daily life.
- By the counsel of others, especially of devout, wise, and experienced men and women of God.
- By deep inward conviction, which increases as we wait upon Him in prayer and readiness to obey. It is by this sovereign conviction that men and women are called to preach, to go to foreign fields as missionaries, and to devote their time, talents, money, and lives to God's work.

Why do people seek for guidance and not find it?

- Because they do not diligently study God's Word and seek to be filled with its truths and principles. They neglect the cultivation of their minds and hearts in the school of Christ, and so miss divine guidance. One of the mightiest men of God now living used to carry his Bible with him into the coal mine when he was only a boy. He spent his spare time filling his mind and heart with its heavenly truths and so prepared himself to be divinely led in mighty labors for God.
- Because they do not humbly accept the daily providences, circumstances, and conditions of their everyday life as a part of God's present plan for them, as His school in which He would

train them for greater things, as His vineyard in which He would have them diligently labor. A young woman imagined she was called to devote herself entirely to saving souls, but under the searching training through which she had to pass, she saw her selfishness and said she would have to return home, live a holy life there, and seek to get her family members into right relationships with God—something she had utterly neglected—before she could go into the work. If we are not faithful at home or in the shop, mill, or place where we work, we shall miss God's way for us.

- Because they are not teachable and are unwilling to receive instruction from other Christians. They are not humble.

- Because they do not wait on God and listen to and heed the inner leadings of the Holy Spirit. They are self-willed. They want their own way. Someone has said, "That which is often asked of God is not so much His will and way, as His approval of our way."[2] And another has said, "God's guidance is plain, when we are true."[3] If we promptly and gladly obey, we shall not miss the way. Paul said, "I was not disobedient unto the heavenly vision" (Acts 26:19 KJV). He obeyed God at all costs, and thus the Holy Spirit could guide him.

- Because of fear and unbelief. It was this fearfulness and unbelief that caused the Israelites to turn back and not go into Canaan when Caleb and Joshua assured them that God would help them to possess the land. They lost sight of God and feared the giants and walled cities, and so missed God's way for them and perished in the wilderness.

- Because they do not take everything promptly and confidently to God in prayer. Paul told us to be "instant in prayer" (Rom. 12:12 KJV), and I am persuaded that it is slowness and delay, sloth and sleepiness in prayer, that rob God's children of the glad assurance of His guidance in all things.

- Because of impatience and haste. Some of God's plans for us unfold slowly, and we must patiently and calmly wait on Him in faith and faithfulness, assured that in due time He will make plain His way for us, if our faith does not fail. It is never God's will that we should get into a headlong hurry but rather that, with patient steadfastness, we should learn to stand still when the pillar of cloud and fire does not move, and that with loving confidence and glad promptness we should strike our tents and march forward when He leads.

> When we cannot see our way,
> Let us trust and still obey;
> He who bids us forward go,
> Cannot fail the way to show.

> Though the sea be deep and wide,
> Though a passage seem denied;
> Fearless, let us still proceed,
> Since the Lord vouchsafes to lead.[4]

Finally, we may rest assured that the Holy Spirit never leads His people to do anything that is wrong or contrary to God's will as revealed in the Bible. He never leads anyone to be impolite and discourteous. "Be courteous" is a divine command (1 Pet. 3:8 KJV). He would have us respect the minor graces of gentle, kindly manners, as well as the great laws of holiness and righteousness.

He may sometimes lead us in ways that are hard for flesh and blood, and that bring to us sorrow and loss in this life. He led Jesus into the wilderness to be sorely tried by the Devil, to Pilate's judgment hall, and to the cross. He led Paul in ways that meant imprisonment, stonings, whippings, hunger and cold, and bitter persecution and death. But He upheld Paul until he cried out, "Most gladly therefore will I rather glory in my infirmities, that the power of Christ may rest upon me. Therefore I take pleasure in infirmities, in reproaches, in necessities, in persecutions, in distresses for Christ's sake" (2 Cor. 12:9–10 KJV). Oh, to be thus led by our heavenly Guide!

He leadeth me! Oh, blessed thought!
Oh, words with heavenly comfort fraught!
Whate'er I do, where'er I be,
Still 'tis God's hand that leadeth me.

Sometimes 'mid scenes of deepest gloom,
Sometimes where Eden's bowers bloom,
By waters still, o'er troubled sea,
Still 'tis God's hand that leadeth me.

Lord, I will clasp Thy hand in mine,

Nor ever murmur nor repine,

Content, whatever lot I see,

Since 'tis my God that leadeth me.

And when my task on earth is done,

When by Thy grace the victory's won,

E'en death's cold wave I will not flee,

Since God through Jordan leadeth me.[5]

NOTES

1. William Williams, "Guide Me, O Thou Great Jehovah," 1745, public domain.

2. Sarah F. Smiley, quoted in Mary Wilder Tileston, *Daily Strength for Daily Needs* (Boston: Roberts Brothers, 1889), 267.

3. F. W. Robertson, ibid.

4. Thomas Kelly, "When We Cannot See Our Way," 1842, public domain.

5. Joseph H. Gilmore, "He Leadeth Me," 1862, public domain.

The Meek and Lowly Heart

I know a man whose daily prayer for years was that he might be meek and lowly in heart as was his Master. "Take my yoke upon you, and learn of me," said Jesus, "for I am meek and lowly in heart" (Matt. 11:29 KJV).

How lowly Jesus was! He was the Lord of life and glory. He made the worlds and upholds them by His word of power. But He humbled Himself, became human, and was born of the virgin in a manger among the cattle. He lived among the common people and worked at the carpenter's bench. And then, anointed with the Holy Spirit, He went about doing good, preaching the gospel to the poor, and ministering to the manifold needs of the sick and sinful and sorrowful. He touched the lepers. He was the friend of sinners. His whole life was a ministry of mercy to those who most needed Him. He humbled Himself to our low estate. He was a King who came "humble, riding on a donkey—

riding on a donkey's colt" (Zech. 9:9 NLT). He was a King, but His crown was of thorns and a cross was His throne.

Paul gave us a picture of the mind and heart of Jesus. He exhorted the Philippians, saying, "Don't be selfish; don't try to impress others. Be humble, thinking of others as better than yourselves" (Phil. 2:3 NLT), and then he added, "You must have the same attitude that Christ Jesus had. 'Though he was God, he did not think of equality with God as something to cling to. Instead, he gave up his divine privileges; he took the humble position of a slave and was born as a human being. When he appeared in human form, he humbled himself in obedience to God and died a criminal's death on a cross'" (Phil. 2:5–8 NLT).

When the Holy Spirit finds His way into a man or woman's heart, the Spirit of Jesus has come to that person and produces the same meekness of heart and lowly service that were seen in the Master. Ambition for place and power and money and fame vanishes, and in its place is a consuming desire to be good and do good, to accomplish in full God's blessed, beneficent will.

Some time ago I met a woman who—as a trained nurse in Paris, nursing rich, English-speaking foreigners—received pay that in a few years would have made her independently wealthy. But the spirit of Jesus came into her heart, and she is now nursing the poor, giving her life to them, doing the most loathsome and exacting service for them, and doing it with a smiling face, for her food and clothes.

Some capable men in one of the largest American cities lost their spiritual balance, cut themselves loose from all other Christians, and made quite a religious stir among many good people for a while. They were very clear and powerful in their presentation of certain phases of truth, but they were also very strong, if not bitter, in their denunciations of all existing religious organizations. They attacked the churches, pointing out so skillfully and with such professions of sanctity what they considered wrong that many people were made most dissatisfied with the churches (including The Salvation Army).

A Salvation Army captain (minister) listened to them and was greatly moved by their fervor, their burning appeals, their religious ecstasy, and their denunciations of the lukewarmness of other Christians. She began to wonder if they were right after all and the Holy Spirit was not among us. Her heart was full of distress, and she cried to God. And then the vision of our slum officers rose before her eyes. She saw their devotion and sacrifice, their lowly, hidden service year after year among the poor and ignorant and vicious, and she said to herself, "Is not this the Spirit of Jesus? Would these men who denounce us so be willing to forgo their religious ecstasies and spend their lives in such lowly, unheralded service?" And the mists that had begun to blind her eyes were swept away, and she saw Jesus still among us going about doing good in the person of our slum officers—and all who for His name's sake sacrifice their time, money, and strength to bless and save others.

Another captain used to slip out of bed early in the morning to pray and then black his own and his assistant's boots, and God mightily blessed him. I saw him recently—now a commissioner with thousands under his command—at an outing in the woods by the lakeshore, looking after poor and forgotten souls and giving them food with his own hand. Like the Lord, his eyes seemed to be in every place beholding opportunities to do good, and his feet and hands always followed his eyes. That is the fruit of the indwelling Holy Spirit.

You who have visions of glory and rapturous delight, and so count yourselves filled with the Spirit, do these visions lead you to virtue and to lowly, loving service? If not, watch yourselves, lest, exalted like Capernaum to heaven, you are at last cast down to hell (see Matt. 11:23). Thank God for the mounts of transfiguration where we behold His glory! But down below in the valley are suffering children, and to them He would have us go with the glory of the mount on our faces, lowly love and vigorous faith in our hearts, and clean hands ready for any service. He would have us give ourselves to them. And if we love Him, if we follow Him, if we are truly filled with the Holy Spirit, we will.

Hope 10

Are you ever cast down and depressed in spirit? Listen to Paul: "I pray that God, the source of hope, will fill you completely with joy and peace because you trust in him. Then you will overflow with confident hope through the power of the Holy Spirit" (Rom. 15:13 NLT). What cheer is in those words! They ring like the shout of a triumph.

God Himself is "the source of hope." There is no gloom, no depression, no wasting sickness of deferred hope in Him. He is a brimming fountain and ocean of hope eternally, and He is our God. He is our hope.

Out of His infinite fullness He is to fill us — not half fill us, but fill us "completely with joy and peace."

And this is not by some condition or means that is so high and difficult that we cannot perform our part, but it is simply by trusting in Him — something the little child and the aged philosopher, the poor and the rich, the ignorant and the learned can do. And the result will be an overflowing "with confident hope through the power of the Holy Spirit."

And what power is that? If it is physical power, then the power of a million Niagaras and flowing oceans and rushing worlds is as nothing compared to it. If it is mental power, then the power of Plato and Bacon and Milton and Shakespeare and Newton is as the light of a firefly to the sun when compared to it. If it is spiritual power, then there is nothing with which it can be compared. But suppose it is all three in one, infinite and eternal! This is the power, throbbing with love and mercy, to which we are to bring our little hearts by living faith, and God will fill us with joy and peace and hope by the incoming of the Holy Spirit.

God's people are a hopeful people. They hope in God, with whom there is no change, no weakness, no decay. In the darkest night and the fiercest storm they still hope in Him, though it may be feebly. But He would have His people "abound in hope" (Rom. 15:13 KJV) so that they should always be buoyant, triumphant.

But how can this be in a world such as this? We are surrounded by awful, mysterious, and merciless forces that may overwhelm us at any moment. The fire may burn us, the water may drown us, the hurricane may sweep us away, friends may desert us, foes may master us. There is the depression that comes from failing health or poverty, from overwork and sleepless nights and constant care, from thwarted plans, disappointed ambitions, slighted love, and base ingratitude. Old age comes on with its gray hairs, failing strength, dimness of sight, dullness of hearing, tottering step, shortness of breath, and general weakness and decay. The friends of youth die, and a new, strange, pushing generation that knows you not comes, elbowing you aside and taking your place. Though in time past some blessed outpouring of the Spirit saw the work of God revive, suffering souls saved, Zion put on her beautiful garments, reforms of all kind advance, the desert blossom as the rose, the waste place become a fruitful field, and the millennium seemed just at hand, the woeful day arrives in which the spiritual tide recedes; the forces of evil are emboldened and they mass themselves and sweep again over the heritage of the Lord, leaving it waste and desolate. And the battle must be fought over again.

How can one be always hopeful, always abounding in hope, in such a world? It is possible only "through the power of the Holy Spirit," and this power will not fail as long as we fix our eyes on eternal things and believe.

The Holy Spirit, dwelling within, turns our eyes from that which is temporal to that which is eternal, from the trial itself to God's purpose in the trial, from the present pain to the precious promise.

I am now writing in a little city made rich by vast potteries. If the dull, heavy clay on the potter's wheel and in the fiery oven could think and speak, it would doubtless cry out against the fierce agony. But if it could foresee the potter's purpose in it, and the thing of use and beauty he meant to make it, it would nestle low under his hand and rejoice in hope.

We are clay in the hand of the divine Potter, but we can think and speak and in some measure understand His high purpose in us. It is the work of the Holy Spirit to make us understand. And if we will not be dull and senseless and unbelieving, He will illuminate us and fill us with peaceful, joyous hope.

He would reveal to us that our heavenly Potter has Himself been on the wheel and in the fiery furnace, learning obedience and being fashioned into "the captain of [our] salvation" (Heb. 2:10 KJV) by the things He suffered. When we are tempted and tried and tempest-tossed, He raises our hope by showing us Jesus suffering and sympathizing with us, tempted in all points as we are, and so able and wise and willing to help us in our struggle and conflict (see Heb. 2:9–18). He assures us that Jesus, into whose hands is committed all power in heaven and earth, is our elder Brother, "touched with the feeling of our infirmities" (Heb. 4:15 KJV), and He encourages us to rest in Him and not be afraid. So we abound in hope through His power as we believe.

He also reveals to us God's eternal purpose in our trials and difficulties. Listen to Paul: "All things work together for good to them that love God" (Rom. 8:28 KJV). "We know this," said Paul. But how can this be? Ah, there is where faith must be exercised. It is in believing that we "overflow with confident hope through the power of the Holy Spirit" (Rom. 15:13 NLT).

God's wisdom and ability to make all things work together for our good are not to be measured by our understanding but firmly held by our faith. My child is in serious difficulty and does not know how to help himself, but I say, "Leave it to me." He may not understand how I am to help him, but he trusts me, and rejoices in hope. We are God's dear children, and He knows how to help us and make all things work together for our good, if we will only commit ourselves to Him in faith.

Thou art as much His care as if beside

Nor man nor angel lived in heaven or earth;

Thus sunbeams pour alike their glorious tide,

To light up worlds, or wake an insect's mirth.[1]

When afflictions overtake us, the Holy Spirit encourages our hope and makes it abound by many promises: "For our present troubles are small and won't last very long. Yet they produce for us a glory that vastly outweighs them and will last forever! So we don't look at the troubles we can see now; rather, we fix our gaze on things that cannot be seen. For the things we see now will soon be gone, but the things we cannot see will last forever" (2 Cor. 4:17–18 NLT).

But such a promise as that only mocks us if we do not believe. "In all their suffering he also suffered, and he personally rescued them. In his love and mercy he redeemed them. He lifted them up and carried them through all the years" (Isa. 63:9 NLT). And He is just the same today. To some He says, "I have refined you in the furnace of suffering" (Isa. 48:10 NLT), and nestling down into His will and believing, they "overflow with confident hope through the power of the Holy Spirit" (Rom. 15:13 NLT).

He turns our eyes back upon Job in his loss and pain, Joseph sold into Egyptian slavery, Daniel in the lions' den, the three Hebrews in the fiery furnace, and Paul in prison and shipwreck and manifold perils. And, showing us their steadfastness and their final triumph, He prompts us to hope in God.

When weakness of body overtakes us, He encourages us with such assurances as these: "My health may fail, and my spirit may grow weak, but God remains the strength of my heart; he is mine forever" (Ps. 73:26 NLT) and, "Though our bodies are dying, our spirits are being renewed every day" (2 Cor. 4:16 NLT).

When old age comes creeping on apace, we can rely on His promise to meet the need, that our hope fail not. The psalmist prayed, "And now, in my old age, don't set me aside. Don't abandon me when my strength is failing. . . . Now that I am old and gray, do not abandon me, O God. Let me proclaim your power to this new generation, your mighty miracles to all who come after me" (Ps. 71:9, 18 NLT).

And through Isaiah the Lord replied, "Even to your old age and gray hairs I am he, I am he who will sustain you. I have made you and I will carry you; I will sustain you and I will rescue you" (Isa. 46:4 NIV).

And David cried out, "But the godly will flourish like palm trees and grow strong like the cedars of Lebanon. For they are transplanted to the LORD's own house. They flourish in the courts of our God. Even in old age they will still produce fruit; they will remain vital and green. They will declare, 'The LORD is just! He is my rock!'" (Ps. 92:12–15 NLT).

The Bible is full of such promises. They have been given by infinite wisdom and love to meet us at every point of doubt and fear and need that, in believing them, we may have a steadfast and glad hope in God. He is pledged to help us. He says, "Don't be afraid, for I am with you. Don't be discouraged, for I am your God. I will strengthen you and help you. I will hold you up with my victorious right hand" (Isa. 41:10 NLT).

When life's waves and billows seemed to sweep over the psalmist, and his soul was bowed within him, three times he cried, "Why am I discouraged? Why is my heart so sad? I will put my hope in God! I will praise him again—my Savior and my God!" (Ps. 42:5 NLT).

And Jeremiah, remembering the wormwood and the gall, and the deep mire of the dungeon into which they had plunged him and from which he had scarcely been delivered, said, "It is good to wait quietly for salvation from the LORD" (Lam. 3:26 NLT).

When the Holy Spirit is come, He brings to remembrance these precious promises and makes them living words. And if we believe, the whole heaven of our soul shall be lit up with abounding hope. It is only through ignorance of God's promises, or through weak and wavering faith, that hope is dimmed. Oh, that we may heed the still small voice of the heavenly Comforter and steadfastly, joyously believe!

My hope is built on nothing less
Than Jesus' blood and righteousness;
When all around my soul gives way,
He then is all my hope and stay.[2]

NOTES

1. John Keble, quoted in Mary Wilder Tileston, *Daily Strength for Daily Needs* (Boston: Roberts Brothers, 1889), 56.

2. Edward Mote, "My Hope Is Built on Nothing Less," 1834, public domain.

The Holy Spirit's Substitute for Gossip and Evil-Speaking 11

The other day I heard a man of God say, "We cannot bridle the tongues of the people among whom we live; they will talk." And by "talk," he meant gossip and criticism and faultfinding.

> You never can tell when you send a word
> Like an arrow shot from a bow
> By an archer blind, be it cruel or kind,
> Just where it will chance to go.
> It may pierce the breast of your dearest friend,
> Tipped with its poison or balm,
> To a stranger's heart in life's great mart
> It may carry its pain or its calm.[1]

The wise mother, when she finds her little boy playing with a sharp knife or looking glass or some dainty dish, does not snatch it away with a slap on his cheek or harsh words, but quietly and gently substitutes a safer and more interesting toy, and so avoids a storm.

A sensible father who finds his boy reading a book of dangerous tendency will kindly point out its character and substitute a better book that is equally interesting.

When children want to spend their evenings on the street, thoughtful and intelligent parents will seek to make their evenings at home more healthfully attractive.

When we seek to rid our minds of evil and hurtful thoughts, we will find it wise to follow Paul's exhortation to the Philippians: "Fix your thoughts on what is true, and honorable, and right, and pure, and lovely, and admirable. Think about things that are excellent and worthy of praise" (Phil. 4:8 NLT). Anyone who faithfully, patiently, and persistently accepts this program of Paul's will find evil thoughts vanishing away.

This is the Holy Spirit's method. He has a pleasant and safe substitute for gossip and faultfinding and slander. Here it is: "Be filled with the Holy Spirit, singing psalms and hymns and spiritual songs among yourselves, and making music to the Lord in your hearts. And give thanks for everything to God the Father in the name of our Lord Jesus Christ" (Eph. 5:18–20 NLT). This is certainly a fruit of being filled with the Spirit.

Many years ago the Lord gave me a blessed revival in a little village in which nearly every soul in the place, as well as farmers from the surrounding country, experienced new life in Christ. One result was that they now had no time for gossip and doubtful talk about their neighbors. They were all talking about religion and rejoicing in the things of the Lord. If they met each other on the street or in some shop or store, they praised the Lord and encouraged each other to press on in the heavenly way. If they met someone who wasn't a Christian, they tenderly besought him or her to be reconciled to God, to give up his or her sins, to "flee from the wrath to come" (Luke 3:7 KJV), and to start at once for heaven. If they met in each other's houses, they gathered around the organ or piano and sang hymns and songs, and did not part until they had united in prayer.

There was no criticizing of their neighbors, no grumbling and complaining about the weather, no faultfinding with their lot in life or their daily surroundings and circumstances. Their conversation was joyous, cheerful, and helpful to one another. Nor was it forced and out of place, but rather it was the natural, spontaneous outflow of loving, humble, glad hearts filled with the Spirit, in union with Jesus, and in love and sympathy with everyone.

This is our heavenly Father's ideal of social and spiritual interaction for His children on earth. He would not have us separate ourselves from each other and shut ourselves up in convents and monasteries in austere asceticism on the one hand, nor would He have us light and foolish, or faultfinding and censorious on the other hand, but sociable, cheerful, and full of tender, considerate love.

On the day of Pentecost, when they were all filled with the Holy Spirit and a multitude came to faith in Christ, we read that they "worshiped together at the Temple each day, met in homes for the Lord's Supper, and shared their meals with great joy and generosity—all the while praising God and enjoying the goodwill of all the people" (Acts 2:46–47 NLT). This is a sample of the brotherly love and unity our heavenly Father would have throughout the whole earth. But how the breath of gossip and evil-speaking would have marred this heavenly fellowship and separated these "chief friends" (Prov. 16:28 KJV).

> Lord! subdue our selfish will;
> Each to each our tempers suit
> By Thy modulating skill,
> Heart to heart, as lute to lute.[2]

However, let no one suppose that the Holy Spirit accomplishes this heavenly work by some overwhelming baptism that does away with the need of our cooperation. He does not override us but works with us, and we must intelligently and determinedly work with Him in this matter.

People often fall into idle and hurtful gossip and evil-speaking not so much from ill-will as from old habit, as a wagon falls into a rut. Or they drift into it with the current of conversation about them. Or they are beguiled into it by a desire to say something and be pleasant and entertaining.

But when the Holy Spirit comes, He lifts us out of the old ruts, and we must follow Him with care lest we fall into them again, possibly never more to escape. He gives us life and power to stem the adverse currents about us, but we must exercise ourselves not to be swept downward by them. He does not destroy the desire to please, but He subordinates it to the desire to help and bless, and we must stir ourselves up to do this.

When Frances Ridley Havergal was asked to sing and play before a worldly company, she sang a sweet song about Jesus and, without displeasing anybody, greatly blessed the company.

At a breakfast party John Fletcher told his experience so sweetly and naturally that all hearts were stirred, the Holy Spirit fell upon the company, and they ended with a glorious prayer meeting. William Bramwell used to steadily and persistently turn the conversation at meals into spiritual channels, to the blessing of all who were present, so that they had two meals—one for the body and one for the soul. To do this wisely and helpfully requires thought and prayer and a fixed purpose—and a tender, loving heart filled with the Holy Spirit. I know a mother who seeks to have a brief season of prayer and a verse of Scripture just before going to dinner to prepare her heart to guide the conversation along spiritual highways.

Are you similarly careful? Do you have victory in this matter? If not, seek it right now in simple, trustful prayer, and the Lord who loves you will surely answer and will be your helper from this time forth. He surely will. Believe right now, and henceforth "conduct yourselves in a manner worthy of the gospel of Christ" (Phil. 1:27 NIV).

I ask Thee, ever blessed Lord,
That I may never speak a word,
Of envy born, or passion stirred.
First, true to Thee in heart and mind,
Then always to my neighbor kind,
By Thy good hand to good inclined.
Oh, save from words that bear a sting,

That pain to any brother bring:

Inbreathe Thy calm in everything.

Let love within my heart prevail,

To rule my words when thoughts assail,

That, hid in Thee, I may not fail.

I know, my Lord, Thy power within

Can save from all the power of sin;

In Thee let every word begin.

Should I be silent? Keep me still,

Glad waiting on my Master's will:

Thy message through my lips fulfill.

Give me Thy words when I should speak,

For words of Thine are never weak,

But break the proud, but raise the meek.

Into Thy lips all grace is poured,

Speak Thou through me, Eternal Word,

Of thought, of heart, of lips the Lord.[3]

NOTES

1. Ella Wheeler Wilcox, "You Never Can Tell," *The Best Loved Poems of the American People*, ed. Hazel Felleman (New York: Doubleday, 1936), 144.

2. Charles Wesley, "Lord, Subdue Our Selfish Will," 1848, public domain.

3. Author unknown, "Speak Thou through Me," *The Herald of Christ's Kingdom* 29, no. 2 (February 1946), n. p.

The Sin against the Holy Spirit 12

God is love, and the Holy Spirit is ceaselessly striving to make this love known in our hearts, to work out God's purposes of love in our lives, and to transform and transfigure our characters by love. And so we are solemnly warned against resisting the Spirit and almost tearfully and always tenderly exhorted to "quench not the Spirit" (1 Thess. 5:19 KJV) and not to "grieve the Holy Spirit of God, by whom you were sealed for the day of redemption" (Eph. 4:30 NKJV).

There is one great sin against which Jesus warned, as a sin never to be forgiven in this world or in that which is to come. That was blasphemy against the Holy Spirit.

That there is such a sin, Jesus taught in Matthew 12:31–32; Mark 3:28–30; and Luke 12:10. And it may be that this is the sin referred to in Hebrews 6:4–6 and 10:29.

Since many of God's dear children have fallen into dreadful distress through fear that they had committed this sin, it may be helpful for us to carefully study what constitutes it.

On one occasion, Jesus was casting out devils, and Mark said that "the teachers of religious law who had arrived from Jerusalem said, 'He's possessed by Satan, the prince of demons. That's where he gets the power to cast out demons'" (Mark 3:22 NLT). To this Jesus replied with gracious kindness and searching logic: "How can Satan cast out Satan? . . . A kingdom divided by civil war will collapse. Similarly, a family splintered by feuding will fall apart. And if Satan is divided and fights against himself, how can he stand? He would never survive. Let me illustrate this further. Who is powerful enough to enter the house of a strong man like Satan and plunder his goods? Only someone even stronger—someone who could tie him up and then plunder his house" (Mark 3:23–27 NLT).

In this quiet reply, we see that Jesus did not rail against them, nor flatly deny their base assertion that He did His miracles by the Devil's power, but showed how logically false their statement was. And then, with grave authority (and I think with solemn tenderness in His voice and eyes), He added, "I tell you the truth, all sin and blasphemy can be forgiven, but anyone who blasphemes the Holy Spirit will never be forgiven. This is a sin with eternal consequences" (Mark 3:28–29 NLT). Then Mark added, "He told them this because they were saying, 'He's possessed by an evil spirit'" (Mark 3:30 NLT).

Jesus came into the world to reveal God's truth and love to people, and to save them, and we are saved by believing in Him. But how could the people of His day—who saw Him working at the carpenter's bench and living the life of an ordinary man of humble toil and daily temptation and trial—believe His stupendous claim to be the only-begotten Son of God, the Savior of the world, and the final Judge of all? Any willful and proud impostor could make such a claim. But people *could* not and *ought* not to believe such an assertion unless the claim was supported by indisputable evidence. This evidence Jesus began to give not only in the holy life He lived and the pure gospel He preached, but also in the blind eyes He opened, the sick He healed, the hungry thousands He fed, the seas He stilled, the dead He raised to life again, and the devils He cast out of bound and harassed souls.

The scribes and Pharisees witnessed these miracles and were compelled to admit these signs and wonders. Nicodemus, one of their number, said to Jesus, "Rabbi . . . we all know that God has sent you to teach us. Your miraculous signs are evidence that God is with you" (John 3:2 NLT). Would they now admit His claim to be the Son of God, their promised and long-looked-for Messiah? They were thoughtful and very religious, but not spiritual. The gospel He preached was Spirit and life; it appealed to their conscience and revealed their sin, and to acknowledge Him was to admit that they themselves were wrong. It meant submission to His authority, the surrender of their wills, and a change of front in their whole inner and outer life. This meant moral and spiritual revolution in every heart and life, and to this they would not submit. And so to avoid such plain inconsistency, they had to discredit His miracles. And since they could not deny them, they declared that He performed them by the Devil's power.

Jesus worked these signs and wonders by the Holy Spirit's power, that He might win their confidence and that they might reasonably believe and become His followers. But they refused to believe, and in their malignant obstinacy heaped scorn upon Him, accusing Him of being in league with the Devil. So how could they be saved? This was the sin against the Holy Spirit against which Jesus warned them. It was not so much one act of sin as a deep-seated, stubborn rebellion against God that led them to choose darkness rather than light, and so to blaspheme against the Spirit of truth and light. It was sin full and ripe and ready for the harvest.

Someone has said,

This sin cannot be forgiven, not because God is unwilling to forgive . . . but because one who thus sins against the Holy Spirit has put himself where no power can soften his heart or change his nature. A man may misuse his eyes and yet see; but whosoever puts them out can never see again. One may misdirect his mariner's compass and turn it aside from the north pole by a magnet or piece of iron, and it may recover and point right again; but whosoever destroys the compass itself has lost his guide at sea.[1]

Many of God's dear children—honest souls—have been persuaded that they have committed this awful sin. Indeed, I once thought that I myself had done so, and for twenty-eight days I felt that, like Jonah, I was in "the belly of hell" (Jon. 2:2 KJV). But God, in love and tender mercy, drew me out of the horrible pit of doubt and fear, and showed me that this is a sin committed only by those who, in spite of all evidence, harden their hearts in unbelief and deny and blaspheme the Lord to shield themselves in their sins. It is a result of willful refusal and rejection of light, and in that direction lies hardness of heart beyond recovery, fullness of sin, and final impenitence, which are unpardonable.

Doubtless many through resistance to the Holy Spirit come to this awful state of heart. But those troubled, anxious souls who think they have committed this sin are not usually among the number.

One night a gentleman arose during a revival in Canada and with deep emotion urged those present to yield themselves to God, accept Jesus as their Savior, and receive the Holy Spirit. He told them that he had once been a Christian, but that he had not walked in the light and consequently had sinned against the Holy Spirit and could nevermore be pardoned. Then, with all earnest tenderness, he exhorted them to be warned by his sad state and not to harden their hearts against the gracious influences, and he entreated them to yield to the Savior. Suddenly the scales of doubt dropped from his eyes, and he saw that he had not in his inmost heart rejected Jesus, and so had not committed the unpardonable sin. He saw that,

The love of God is broader
Than the measure of man's mind:
And the heart of the Eternal
Is most wonderfully kind.[2]

In an instant his heart was filled with light and love and peace and sweet assurance that Christ Jesus was his Savior.

I have known three people—in one meeting—who thought they had committed this sin, and who, bowed with grief and fear, came to the penitent form (the kneeler in the church where forgiveness is sought) to find deliverance.

The English poet William Cowper was plunged into unutterable gloom by the conviction that he had committed this awful sin. But God tenderly brought him into the light and sweet comforts of the Holy Spirit again, and doubtless it was in the sense of such loving-kindness that he wrote:

> There is a fountain filled with blood,
> Drawn from Emanuel's veins;
> And sinners plunged beneath that flood
> Lose all their guilty stains.[3]

John Bunyan was also afflicted with horrible fears that he had committed this sin. In *Grace Abounding to the Chief of Sinners* (a book I earnestly recommend to all), he tells how he was delivered from his doubts and was filled once more with the joy of the Lord. There are portions of his book *The Pilgrim's Progress* that should be interpreted in the light of this grievous experience.

Those who think they have committed this sin may generally be assured that they have not. Their hearts are usually very tender, while this sin must harden the heart past all feeling. They are full of sorrow and shame for having neglected God's grace and trifled with the Savior's dying words, but such sorrow could not exist in a heart so fully given over to sin that pardon was impossible. God says, "Whosoever will may come" (see Rev. 22:17). So if they find it in their hearts to come, they will not be cast out but freely pardoned and received with loving-kindness through the merits of Jesus' blood. God's promise will not fail. His faithfulness is established in the heavens. Those who have committed this sin are full of evil, do not care to come, and will not, and therefore are never pardoned. Their sin is eternal.

NOTES

1. F. N. Peloubet, *The Teachers' Commentary on the Gospel According to St. Matthew* (New York: Oxford University Press, 1901), 153.

2. Frederick W. Faber, "There's a Wideness in God's Mercy," 1854, public domain

3. William Cowper, "There Is a Fountain Filled with Blood," 1772, public domain.

Offenses against the Holy Spirit 13

One day in a fit of boyish temper, I spoke hot words of anger—somewhat unjustly—against another person, and this deeply grieved my mother. She said little, and though her sweet face has moldered many years beneath the Southern daisies, I can still see her look of grief across the years of a third of a century. That is the one sad memory of my childhood. A stranger might have been amused or incensed at my words, but Mother was grieved—grieved to her heart by my lack of generous, self-forgetful, thoughtful love.

We can anger a stranger or an enemy, but it is only a friend we grieve. The Holy Spirit is such a friend, more tender and faithful than a mother. And shall we carelessly offend Him and estrange ourselves from Him in spite of His love?

There is a sense in which every sin is against the Holy Spirit. Of course, not every such sin is unpardonable, but the tendency of all sin is in that direction, and we are only safe as we avoid the very beginnings of sin. Only as we "walk in the Spirit" are we "free from the law of sin and death" (Rom. 8:2 KJV). Therefore, it is infinitely important that we be aware of offenses against the Spirit, "lest any of you be hardened through the deceitfulness of sin" (Heb. 3:13 KJV).

Grieving the Holy Spirit is a very common and sad offense of professing Christians, and it is to this that much of the weakness and ignorance and joylessness of so many followers of Christ must be attributed.

Jesus is grieved, as was my mother, by the unloving speech and spirit of God's children. Paul, in his letters to the Ephesians, said, "Don't use foul or abusive language. Let everything you say be good and helpful, so that your words will be an encouragement to those who hear them." And then he added,

And do not bring sorrow to God's Holy Spirit by the way you live. Remember, he has identified you as his own, guaranteeing that you will be saved on the day of redemption. Get rid of all bitterness, rage, anger, harsh words, and slander, as well as all types of evil behavior. Instead, be kind to each other, tenderhearted, forgiving one another, just as God through Christ has forgiven you. Imitate God, therefore, in everything you do, because you are his dear children. Live a life filled with love, following the example of Christ. He loved us and offered himself as a sacrifice for us, a pleasing aroma to God. (Eph. 4:29—5:2 NLT)

What does Paul teach us here? That it is not by some huge wickedness, some Judas-like betrayal, some tempting and lying to the Holy Spirit as Ananias and Sapphira did (see Acts 5:1–9) that we grieve Him, but by that which most people count little and unimportant: by talk that corrupts instead of blessing and building up those that hear, by gossip, by bitterness, and by uncharitable criticisms and faultfindings. This was the sin of the elder son when the prodigal returned, and it was by this he pierced with grief the kind old father's heart (see Luke 15:11–32).

We grieve Him by getting in a rage; by loud, angry talking and evil-speaking and petty malice; by unkindness and hard-heartedness and an unforgiving spirit. We grieve Him by not walking through the world as in our Father's house and among our neighbors and friends as though among His dear children, by not loving tenderly and making kindly sacrifices for one another. And this is not a matter of little importance. It may have sadly momentous consequences.

It is a bitter, cruel, and often irreparable thing to trifle with a valuable earthly friendship. How much more when the friendship is heavenly— when the friend is our Lord and Savior, our Creator and Redeemer, our Governor and Judge, our Teacher, Guide, and God? When we trifle with a friend's wishes—especially when such wishes are all in perfect harmony with and for our highest possible good—we may not estrange the friend from us, but we estrange ourselves from our friend. Our hearts grow cold toward him or her, though his or her heart may be breaking with longing toward us. The more Saul ill-treated David, the more he hated David.

Such estrangement may lead little by little to yet greater sin, to strange hardness of heart, to doubts and unbelief and denial of the Lord.

The cure for all this is a clean heart full of sweet, gentle, self-forgetful, generous love. Then we shall be "followers of God, as dear children," then we shall "walk in love, as Christ . . . loved us, and [gave] himself for us" (Eph. 5:1–2 KJV).

But there is another offense—that of quenching the Spirit—which accounts for the comparative darkness and deadness of many of God's children.

In 1 Thessalonians 5:16–19, the apostle said, "Always be joyful. Never stop praying. Be thankful in all circumstances, for this is God's will for you who belong to Christ Jesus. Do not stifle the Holy Spirit" (NLT).

When will the Lord's dear children learn that the religion of Jesus is a lowly thing and that it is the little foxes that spoil the vines? Does not the apostle here teach that it is not by some desperate, dastardly deed that we quench the Spirit, but simply by neglecting to rejoice and pray and give thanks at all times and for all things?

It is not necessary to blot the sun out of the heavens to keep the sunlight out of your house—just close the blinds and draw the curtains. Nor do you pour barrels of water on the flames to quench the fire—just shut off the draft. Nor do you dynamite the city reservoir and destroy all the mains and pipes to cut off your supply of sparkling water, but just refrain from turning on the main.

So you do not need to do some great evil, some deadly sin, to quench the Spirit. Just cease to rejoice, through fear of human opinion and of being peculiar; be prim and proper as a white and polished gravestone; let gushing joy be curbed; neglect to pray when you feel a gentle pull in your heart to get alone with the Lord; omit giving hearty thanks for all God's tender mercies, faithful discipline, and loving chastening, and soon you will find the Spirit quenched. He will no longer spring up joyously like a well of living water within you.

But give the Spirit a vent, an opening, a chance, and He will rise within you and flood your soul with light and love and joy.

Some years ago a sanctified woman of clear experience went alone to keep her daily hour with God. But, to her surprise, it seemed that she could not find Him, either in prayer or in His Word. She searched her heart for evidence of sin, but the Spirit showed her nothing contrary to God in her mind, heart, or will. She searched her memory for any breach of covenant, any broken vows, any neglect, any omission, but could find none.

Then she asked the Lord to show her if there were any duty unfulfilled, any command unnoticed, which she might perform, and quick as thought came the often-read words, "Rejoice evermore" (1 Thess. 5:16 KJV). "Have you done that this morning?"

She had not. It had been a busy morning, and a well-spent one, but so far there had been no definite rejoicing in her heart, though the manifold riches and ground for joy of all Christians were hers.

At once she began to count her blessings and thank the Lord for each one, and to rejoice in Him for all the ways He had led her and the gifts He had bestowed, and in a very few minutes the Lord stood revealed to her spiritual consciousness.

She had not committed sin, nor resisted the Spirit, but a failure to rejoice in Him who had daily loaded her with benefits had in a measure quenched the Spirit. She had not turned on the main, and so her soul was not flooded with living waters. She had not remembered the command, "Rejoice before the LORD your God in all that you undertake" (Deut. 12:18 ESV). But that morning she learned a lifelong lesson, and she has ever since safeguarded her soul by obeying the many commands to "Rejoice in the Lord" (Phil. 4:4 KJV).

Grieving and quenching the Spirit will not only leave an individual soul barren and desolate, but it will do so for a church, community, whole nation, or continent. We see this illustrated on a large scale by the long and weary Dark Ages, when the light of the gospel was almost extinguished, and only here and there was the darkness broken by the torch of truth held aloft by some humble, suffering soul that had wept and prayed and through painful struggles had found the light.

We see it also in those churches, communities, and countries where revivals are unknown, or are a thing of the past, where souls are not born into the kingdom, and where there is no joyous shout of victory among the people of God.

Grieving and quenching the Spirit may be done unintentionally by lack of thought and prayer and hearty devotion to the Lord Jesus, but they prepare the way and lead to intentional and positive resistance to the Spirit. To resist the Spirit is to fight against Him.

The person who listens to the gospel invitation and—convicted of sin—refuses to submit to God in true repentance and faith in Jesus is resisting the Holy Spirit. We have bold and striking historical illustrations of the danger of resisting the Holy Spirit in the disasters that befell Pharaoh and the terrible calamities that came upon Jerusalem.

The ten plagues that came upon Pharaoh and his people were ten opportunities and open doors into God's favor and fellowship, which they themselves shut by their stubborn resistance, only to be over-taken by dreadful catastrophe.

To the Jewish leaders in Jerusalem, Stephen said, "You always resist the Holy Spirit!" (Acts 7:51 NIV). And the siege and fall of Jerusalem, the butchery and banishment and enslavement of its inhabitants, and all the woes that came upon that city's people, fol-lowed their rejection of Jesus and the hardness of heart and spiritual blindness which swiftly overtook them when they resisted all the lov-ing efforts and entreaties of His disciples baptized with the Holy Spirit.

And what befalls nations and people also befalls individuals. Those who receive and obey the Lord are enlightened and blessed and saved; those who resist and reject Him are sadly left to themselves and surely swallowed up in destruction.

Likewise, professing Christians who hear of heart-holiness and cleansing from all sin as a blessing they may now have by faith and—convicted of their need of the blessing and of God's desire and will-ingness to bestow it upon them now—refuse to seek it in wholehearted affectionate consecration and faith, are resisting the Holy Spirit. And such resistance imperils the soul beyond all possible computation.

We see an example of this in the Israelites who were brought out of Egypt with signs and wonders and led through the Red Sea and the wilderness to the borders of Canaan but, forgetting, refused to go over into the land. In this they resisted the Holy Spirit in His leadings as surely as Pharaoh did, and with quite as disastrous results to them-selves, perishing in their evil way. For their sin was much greater than his as their light exceeded his.

Hundreds of years later, a prophet, writing of this time, said, "In all their suffering he also suffered, and he personally rescued them. In his love and mercy he redeemed them. He lifted them up and carried them through all the years. But they rebelled against him and grieved his Holy Spirit. So he became their enemy and fought against them" (Isa. 63:9–10 NLT).

We see from this that Christians must beware and watch and pray and walk softly with the Lord in glad obedience and childlike faith if they would escape the darkness and dryness that result from grieving and quenching the Spirit and the dangers that surely come from resisting Him.

Arm me with jealous care,
As in Thy sight to live;
And, O, Thy servant, Lord, prepare,
A strict account to give.

Help me to watch and pray,
And on Thyself rely,
Assured if I my trust betray,
I shall forever die.[1]

NOTE

1. Charles Wesley, "A Charge to Keep I Have," 1762, public domain.

The Holy Spirit and Sound Doctrine

14

Is Jesus Christ divine? Is the Bible an inspired book? Are we fallen creatures who can be saved only through the suffering and sacrifice of the Creator? Will there be a resurrection of the dead and a day in which God will judge the world by the Man, Christ Jesus? Is Satan a personal being, and is there a hell in which the wicked will be forever punished?

These are great doctrines that have been held and taught by the followers of Christ since the days of Jesus and His apostles, and yet they are ever being attacked and denied.

Are they true? Or are they only fancies and falsehoods, or figures of speech and distortions of truth? How can we find truth and know it? Jesus said, "When he, the Spirit of truth, is come, he will guide you into all truth" (John 16:13 KJV).

What truth? Not the truth of the multiplication table, or of physical science, or art, or secular history, but spiritual truth—the truth about

God, His will and character, and our relations to Him in Christ, that truth which is necessary to salvation and holiness. Into all this truth the Holy Spirit will guide us. "He shall teach you all things," said Jesus (John 14:26 KJV).

How, then, shall we escape error and be sound in doctrine? Only by the Holy Spirit's help. How do we know Jesus Christ is divine? Because the Bible tells us so? Infinitely precious and important is this revelation in the Bible, but not by this do we know it. Because the church teaches it in its creed and we have heard it from the catechism? Nothing taught in any creed or catechism is of more vital importance, but neither by this do we know it.

How then? Listen to Paul: "No one can say Jesus is Lord, except by the Holy Spirit" (1 Cor. 12:3 NLT). "No one," said Paul. Then learning it from the Bible or catechism is not to know it except as the parrot might know it, but all are to be taught this by the Holy Spirit, if they are to really know it.

Then it is not a revelation made once for all, and only to those who walked and talked with Jesus, but it is a spiritual revelation made anew to each believing heart that in penitence seeks Him and so meets the conditions of such a revelation.

Then the poor, ignorant outcast at The Salvation Army penitent form in the slums of London or Chicago who never heard of a creed and the primitive villager who never saw the inside of a Bible may have Christ revealed in them, and know by the revelation of the Holy Spirit that Jesus is Lord.

"It pleased God . . . to reveal his Son in me," wrote Paul (Gal. 1:15–16 KJV), who also said, "Christ lives in me" (Gal. 2:20 NLT). He wrote to the Galatians, "My dear children, for whom I am again in the pains of childbirth until Christ is formed in you" (Gal. 4:19 NIV), as though Christ is to be spiritually formed in the heart of each believer by the operation of the Holy Spirit, as He was physically formed in the womb of Mary by the same Spirit (see Luke 1:35). And again: "The mystery hidden for ages and generations but now revealed to his saints . . . is Christ in you, the hope of glory" (Col. 1:26–27 ESV). "That Christ may dwell in your hearts by faith" (Eph. 3:17 KJV). "Examine yourselves to see whether you are in the faith; test yourselves. Do you not realize that Christ Jesus is in you—unless, of course, you fail the test" (2 Cor. 13:5 NIV).

"When I am raised to life again," said Jesus, when making His great promise of the Comforter to His disciples, "you will know that I am in my Father, and you are in me, and I am in you" (John 14:20 NLT). And in His Great Priestly Prayer, He said, "I have revealed you to them, and I will continue to do so. Then your love for me will be in them, and I will be in them" (John 17:26 NLT).

It is this ever-recurring revelation to penitent, believing hearts, by the agency of the ever-present Holy Spirit, that makes faith in Jesus Christ living and invincible. "I know He is Lord, for He saves my soul from sin, and He saves me now," is an argument that rationalism and unbelief cannot answer nor overthrow, and as long as there are men and women in the world who can say this, faith in the divinity of Jesus Christ is secure. And this experience and witness come by the Holy Spirit.

I worship Thee, O Holy Ghost,

I love to worship Thee;

My risen Lord for aye were lost

But for Thy company.[1]

And so it is by the guidance and teaching of the Holy Spirit that all saving truth becomes vital to us.

It is He who makes the Bible a living book, He who convinces the world of judgment (see John 16:8–11), He who makes us certain there is a heaven of surpassing and enduring glory and joy and a hell of endless sorrow and woe for those who sin away their day of grace and die in impenitence.

Who have been the mightiest and most faithful preachers of the gloom and terror and pain of a perpetual hell? Those who have been the mightiest and most effective preachers of God's compassionate love.

In all periods of great revival, when men and women seemed to live on the borderland and in the vision of eternity, hell has been preached. The leaders in these revivals have been people of prayer and faith and consuming love, but they have also been people who knew the terrors of the Lord (see Job 6:4) and therefore preached the judgments of God. And they proved that the law with its penalties is a schoolmaster to bring souls to Christ (see Gal. 3:24). Fox the Quaker, Bunyan the Baptist, Baxter the Puritan, Wesley and Fletcher and Whitefield and Caughey the Methodists, Finney the Presbyterian, Edwards and Moody the Congregationalists, and William Booth the Salvationist have preached it—not savagely, but tenderly and faithfully, as a mother might warn her child against some great danger that would surely follow careless and selfish wrongdoing.

Who have loved and labored and sacrificed as these have? Their hearts have been a flaming furnace of love and devotion to God and an overflowing fountain of love and compassion for souls. But just in proportion as they have discovered God's love and pity for humanity, so have they discovered His wrath against sin and all obstinate wrongdoing. And as they have caught glimpses of heaven and declared its joys and everlasting glories, so they have seen hell with its endless punishment, and with trembling voice and overflowing eyes have they warned people to "flee from the wrath to come" (Matt. 3:7 KJV).

Were these preachers, throbbing with spiritual life and consumed with devotion to the kingdom of God and the everlasting well-being of their fellow human beings, led to this belief by the Spirit of truth, or were they misled?

"The things of the Spirit . . . are spiritually discerned," said Paul (1 Cor. 2:14 KJV). It is not by searching and philosophizing that these things are found out, but by revelation. "Flesh and blood has not revealed this to you," said Jesus to Peter, "but my Father who is in heaven" (Matt. 16:17 ESV). The great teacher of truth is the Spirit of truth, and the only safe expounders and guardians of sound doctrine are men and women filled with the Holy Spirit.

Study and research have their place, and an important place. But in spiritual things they will be no avail unless prosecuted by spiritual men and women. As well might someone blind from birth attempt to study the starry heavens and someone born deaf undertake to expound and criticize the harmonies of Bach and Beethoven. We must see and hear if we are to speak and write intelligently on such subjects. And so we must be spiritually enlightened to understand spiritual truth.

The greatest danger to any religious organization is that people should arise in its ranks and hold its positions of trust who have learned its great fundamental doctrines by rote, but have no experiential knowledge of their truth inwrought by the mighty anointing of the Holy Spirit, and who are destitute of "an anointing from the Holy One," which, said John, "teaches you about all things" (1 John 2:20, 27 NIV).

Why do people deny the divinity of Jesus Christ? Because they have never placed themselves in that relation to the Spirit and met those unchanging conditions that would enable Him to reveal Jesus to them as Savior and Lord.

Why do people dispute the inspiration of the Scriptures? Because the Holy Spirit, who inspired "holy men of God" to write the Book (2 Pet. 1:21 KJV), hides its spiritual sense from unspiritual and unholy men and women.

Why do people doubt a day of judgment and a state of everlasting doom? Because they have never been bowed and broken and crushed beneath the weight of their sin and by a sense of guilt and separation from a holy God that can only be removed by faith in His dying Son.

A horseman lost his way in a pitiless storm on a black and starless night. Suddenly his horse drew back and refused to take another step. He urged it forward, but it only threw itself back upon its haunches. Just then a vivid flash of lightning revealed a great precipice upon the brink of which he stood. It was but an instant, and then the pitchy blackness hid it again from view. But he turned his horse and anxiously rode away from the terrible danger.

A distinguished professor of religion said to me some time ago, "I dislike, I abhor, the doctrine of hell." And then after a while he added, "But three times in my life I have seen that there was eternal separation from God and an everlasting hell for me, if I walked not in the way God was calling me to go."

Into the blackness of the sinning soul's night the Holy Spirit, who is patiently and compassionately seeking the salvation of all humanity, flashes a light that gives a glimpse of eternal things which, heeded, would lead to the sweet peace and security of eternal day. For when the Holy Spirit is heeded and honored, the night passes; the shadows flee; the day dawns; the Sun of Righteousness arises with healing in His wings (see Mal. 4:2); and men and women, saved and sanctified, walk in His light in safety and joy. Doctrines which before were repellent and foolishness to the carnal mind or a stumbling block to the heart of unbelief now become precious and satisfying to the soul, and truths which before were hid in impenetrable darkness or seen only as through dense gloom and fog are now seen clearly as in the light of broad day.

> Hold thou the faith that Christ is Lord,
> God over all, who died and rose;
> And everlasting life bestows
> On all who hear the Living Word.
> For thee His life blood He out-poured,
> His Spirit sets thy spirit free;
> Hold thou the faith—He dwells in thee,
> And thou in Him, and Christ is Lord![2]

NOTES

1. William Warren, "I Worship Thee, O Holy Ghost," 1877, public domain.

2. Source unknown.

Praying in the Spirit 15

An important work of the Holy Spirit is to teach us how to pray, instruct us what to pray for, and inspire us to pray earnestly without ceasing—and in faith—for the things we desire and the things that are dear to the Lord's heart. In a familiar verse, the poet James Montgomery said:

> Prayer is the burden of a sigh,
> The falling of a tear,
> The upward glancing of the eye,
> When none but God is near.[1]

And no doubt he is right. Prayer is exceedingly simple. The faintest cry for help, a whisper for mercy, is prayer. But when the Holy Spirit comes and fills the soul with His blessed presence, prayer becomes more than a cry. It ceases to be a feeble request and often becomes a strife (see Rom. 15:30; Col. 4:12) for greater things, a conflict, an invincible argument, a wrestling with God, and through it men and women enter into the divine councils and rise into a blessed and responsible fellowship in some important sense with the Father and the Son in the moral government of the world.

It was in this spirit and fellowship that Abraham prayed for Sodom (see Gen. 18:23–32), that Moses interceded for Israel and stood between them and God's hot displeasure (see Ex. 32:7–14), and that Elijah prevailed to shut up the heavens for three years and six months, and then again prevailed in his prayer for rain (see 1 Kings 17–18).

God would have us come to Him not only as a foolish and ignorant child comes, but as an ambassador to His home government, as a full-grown son who has become of age and entered into partnership with his father, as a bride who is one in all interests and affections with the bridegroom.

He would have us "come boldly unto the throne of grace" (Heb. 4:16 KJV) with a well-reasoned and scriptural understanding of what we desire, and with a purpose to ask, seek, and knock (see Matt. 7:7) till we get the thing we wish, being assured that it is according to His will. And this boldness is not inconsistent with the profoundest humility and a sense of utter dependence. Indeed, it is always accompanied by self-distrust and humble reliance upon the merits of Jesus, or else it is merely presumption and unsanctified conceit. This union of assurance and humility, of boldness and dependence, can be secured only by the baptism with the Holy Spirit, and only so can one be prepared and fitted for such prayer.

Three great obstacles hinder mighty prayer: selfishness, unbelief, and the darkness of ignorance and foolishness. The baptism with the

Spirit sweeps away these obstacles and brings in the three great essentials to prayer: faith, love (divine love), and the light of heavenly knowledge and wisdom.

Selfishness must be cast out by the incoming of love. The ambassador must not be seeking personal ends, but the interests of the government and people he or she represents. The son must not be seeking private gain, but the common prosperity of the partnership in which he will fully and lawfully share. The bride must not forget him to whom she belongs, and seek separate ends, but in all ways identify herself with her husband and his interests. So the child of God must come in prayer, unselfishly.

It is the work of the Holy Spirit, with our cooperation and glad consent, to search and destroy selfishness out of our hearts and fill them with pure love for God and others. And when this is done we shall not then be asking selfishly, to please ourselves and gratify our appetites, pride, ambition, ease, or vanity (see James 4:3). We shall seek only our Lord's glory and the common good of our fellow human beings, in which, as coworkers and partners, we shall have a common share.

If we ask for success, it is not that we may be exalted but that God may be glorified, that Jesus may secure the purchase of His blood, that others may be saved, and that the kingdom of heaven be established upon earth. If we ask for daily bread, it is not that we may be full but that we may be fitted for daily duty. If we ask for health, it is not only that we may be free from pain and filled with physical comfort but that we may be spent "in publishing the sinner's Friend,"[2] in fulfilling the work for which God has placed us here.

Unbelief must be destroyed. Doubt paralyzes prayer. Unbelief quenches the spirit of intercession. Only as the eye of faith sees our Father God upon the throne guaranteeing to us rights and privileges by the blood of His Son—and inviting us to come without fear and make our wants known—does prayer rise from the commonplace to the sublime. Only then does it cease to be a feeble, timid cry, and become a mighty spiritual force, moving God Himself in the interests it seeks.

Those who are wise with the wisdom of this world but poor and naked and blind and foolish in matters of faith ask, "Will God change His plans at the request of mere men and women?" And we answer, "Yes," since many of God's plans are made contingent upon the prayers of His people, and He has ordered that prayer offered in faith, according to His will, revealed in His Word, shall be one of the controlling factors in His government of men and women.

Is it God's will that the tides of the Atlantic and Pacific should sweep across the Isthmus of Panama? That tunnels should run under the Alps? That thoughts and words should be winged across the ocean without any visible or tangible medium? Yes. It is His will, if people will it and work to those ends in harmony with His great physical laws. So in the spiritual world there are wonders produced by prayer, and God wills the will of His people when they come to Him in faith and love.

What else is meant by such promises and assurances as these: "I tell you, you can pray for anything, and if you believe that you've received it, it will be yours" (Mark 11:24 NLT). "The earnest prayer of a righteous person has great power and produces wonderful results. Elijah was as human as we are, and yet when he prayed earnestly that no rain would fall, none fell for three and a half years! Then, when he prayed again, the sky sent down rain and the earth began to yield its crops" (James 5:16–18 NLT).

The Holy Spirit dwelling within the heart helps us to understand the things we may pray for, and the heart that is full of love and loyalty to God wants only what is lawful. This is mystery to people who are under the dominion of selfishness and the darkness of unbelief, but it is a soul-thrilling fact to those who are filled with the Holy Spirit.

"What do you want me to do for you?" asked Jesus of the blind man (Luke 18:41 NLT). He respected the will of the blind man, and granted his request, seeing he had faith. And He still respects the vigorous, sanctified will of His people—the will that has been subdued by consecration and faith into loving union with His will.

The Lord answered Abraham on behalf of Sodom till he ceased to ask (see Gen. 18:16–33). "The Lord has had his way so long with Hudson Taylor," said a friend, "that now, Hudson Taylor can have his way with the Lord."

Adoniram Judson lay sick with a fatal illness in faraway Burma. His wife read to him an account of the conversion of a number of Jews in Constantinople through some of his writings. For a while, the sick man was silent, and then he spoke with awe, telling his wife that for years he had prayed that he might be used in some way to bless the Jews, yet had never seen any evidence that his prayers were answered. But now, after many years and from far away, the evidence of answer had come. And then, after further silence, he spoke with deep emotion, saying that he had never prayed a prayer for the glory of God and the good of others but that, sooner or later (even though for the time being he had forgotten), he found that God had not forgotten but had remembered and patiently worked to answer his prayer.

Oh, the faithfulness of God! He means it when He makes promises and exhorts and urges and commands us to pray. It is not His purpose to mock us, but to answer and "to do exceeding abundantly above all that we ask or think" (Eph. 3:20 KJV).

Knowledge and wisdom must take the place of foolish ignorance. Paul said, "We don't know what God wants us to pray for," and then added, "but the Holy Spirit prays for us with groanings that cannot be expressed in words" (Rom. 8:26 NLT). If my little child asks for a glittering razor, I refuse the request; but when my full-grown son asks for one I grant it. So God cannot wisely answer some prayers, for they are foolish or untimely. Hence, we need not only love and have faith, but also have wisdom and knowledge that we may ask according to God's will.

It is this that Paul had in mind when he said that he would not only pray with the Spirit, but "pray with the understanding also" (1 Cor. 14:15 KJV). We should think before we pray, and study that we may pray wisely.

When the Holy Spirit comes, there pours into the soul not only a tide of love and simple faith, but a flood of light as well, and prayer becomes not only earnest, but intelligent also. And this intelligence increases as, under the leadership of the Holy Spirit, the Word of God is studied and its heavenly truths and principles are grasped and assimilated.

Thus we may come to know God and become His friends, whose prayers He will assist and not deny. Then we will talk with God as friend with friend, and the Holy Spirit will help our infirmities, encourage us to urge our prayer in faith, teach us to reason with God, enable us to come boldly in the name of Jesus—even when oppressed with a sense of our own insignificance and unworthiness—and, when words fail us and we scarcely know how to voice our desires, He will intercede within us with unutterable groanings, according to the will of God (see Rom. 8:26–27; 1 Cor. 2:11).

A young man felt called to mission work in China, but his mother offered strong opposition to his going. An agent of the mission, knowing the need of the work and vexed with the mother, one day laid the case before Hudson Taylor.

He said, "Mr. Taylor listened patiently and lovingly to all I had to say, and then gently suggested our praying about it. Such a prayer I have never heard before! It seemed to me more like a conversation with a trusted friend whose advice he was seeking. He talked the matter over with the Friend from every point of view—from the side of the young man, from the side of China's needs, from the side of the mother and her natural feelings, and also from my side. It was a revelation to me. I saw that prayer did not mean merely asking for things—much less asking for things to be carried out by God according to our ideas—but that it means communion, fellowship, partnership with our heavenly Father. And when our will is really blended with His, what liberty we may have in asking for what we want!"

My soul, ask what thou wilt,
Thou canst not be too bold;
Since His own blood for thee He spilt,
What else can He withhold?[3]

NOTES

1. James Montgomery, "Prayer Is the Soul's Sincere Desire," 1818, public domain.

2. Charles Wesley, "Give Me the Faith Which Can Remove," 1749, public domain.

3. John Newton, "Behold, the Throne of Grace," 1779, public domain.

Characteristics of the Anointed Preacher 16

Since God saves men and women by "the foolishness of preaching" (1 Cor. 1:21 KJV), preachers have an infinitely important work, and they must be fitted for it. But what can fit a person for such sacred work? Not education alone, nor knowledge of books, nor gifts of speech, nor winsome manners, nor a magnetic voice, nor a commanding presence, but only God. Preachers must be more than themselves—they must be themselves plus the Holy Spirit.

Paul was such a man. He was full of the Holy Spirit, and in studying his life and ministry we get a life-sized portrait of an anointed preacher living, fighting, preaching, praying, suffering, triumphing, and dying in the power and light and glory of the indwelling Spirit.

In the second chapter of 1 Thessalonians, he gave us a picture of his character and ministry (which were formed and inspired by the

Holy Spirit), a sample of his workmanship, and an example for all gospel preachers.

At Philippi he had been terribly beaten with stripes on his bare back, he had been roughly thrust into the inner dungeon, and his feet were made fast in the stocks, but that did not break nor quench his spirit. Love burned in his heart, and his joy in the Lord brimmed full and bubbled over. And at midnight, in the damp, dark, loathsome dungeon, he and Silas, his companion in service and suffering, "prayed, and sang praises unto God" (Acts 16:25 KJV). God answered with an earthquake, and the jailer and his household entered the kingdom of God. Paul was set free and went at once to Thessalonica, where— regardless of the shameful way he had been treated at Philippi—he preached the gospel boldly, and a blessed revival followed with many people experiencing new life in Christ. But persecution arose, and Paul had to flee again. His heart, however, was continually turning back to the new Christians there, and at last he sat down and wrote them their letter. From this we learn the following.

He was a joyful preacher. He was no pessimist, croaking out doleful prophecies and lamentations and bitter criticisms. He was full of the joy of the Lord. It was not the joy that comes from good health, a pleasant home, plenty of money, wholesome food, numerous and smiling friends, and sunny, favorable skies, but a deep, springing fountain of solemn, gladdening joy that abounded and overflowed in pain and weariness, in filthy, noisome surroundings, in loneliness and poverty, and in danger and bitter persecutions. No earth-born trial could quench it, for it was heaven-born; it was "the joy of the LORD" (Neh. 8:10 KJV) poured into his heart with the Holy Spirit.

He was a bold preacher. After his experience at Philippi, worldly prudence would have constrained Paul to go softly at Thessalonica, lest he arouse opposition and meet again with personal violence. But instead he said, "Yet our God gave us the courage to declare his Good News to you boldly, in spite of great opposition" (1 Thess. 2:2 NLT). Personal considerations were all forgotten or cast to the winds in his impetuous desire to declare the gospel and save their souls. He lived in the will of God and conquered his fears. "The wicked" are fearful and "run away when no one is chasing them, but the godly are as bold as lions" (Prov. 28:1 NLT).

This boldness is a fruit of righteousness, and is always found in those who are full of the Holy Spirit. They forget themselves, and so lose all fear. This was the secret of the martyrs when burned at the stake or thrown to the wild beasts.

Fear is a fruit of selfishness. Boldness thrives when selfishness is destroyed. God esteems it, commands His people to be courageous, and makes spiritual leaders only of those who possess courage (see Josh. 1:9).

Moses did not fear the wrath of the king, refused to be called the son of Pharaoh's daughter, and boldly espoused the cause of his despised and enslaved people. Joshua was full of courage. Gideon fearlessly attacked one hundred twenty thousand Midianites with just three hundred unarmed men. Jonathan and his armor-bearer charged the Philistine garrison and routed hundreds singlehanded. David faced the lion and the bear, and inspired all Israel by battling with and killing Goliath.

The prophets were men and women of the highest courage, who fearlessly rebuked kings, and at the risk of life (and often at the cost of life) denounced popular sins and called the people back to right-eousness and the faithful service of God. They feared God and so lost the fear of people. They believed God and so obeyed Him, found His favor, and were entrusted with His high missions and everlasting employments.

"Don't be afraid, for I am with you," the Lord said (Isa. 41:10 NLT). The apostle Paul believed this, and so was able to say, "We were bold in our God" (1 Thess. 2:2 NKJV). God was Paul's high tower, his strength and unfailing defense, and so he was not afraid.

His boldness toward people was a fruit of his boldness toward God. That, in turn, was a fruit of Paul's faith in Jesus as his High Priest, who understood his weaknesses, and through whom he could "come boldly unto the throne of grace . . . [to] obtain mercy, and find grace to help in time of need" (Heb. 4:16 KJV).

It is the timidity and delicacy with which people attempt God's work that often accounts for their failure. Let them speak out boldly, as ambassadors of heaven who are not afraid to represent their King, and they will command attention and respect and reach the hearts and consciences of those who hear them.

I have read that Bishop Hugh Latimer, who was later burned at the stake, having preached a sermon before King Henry VIII which greatly displeased the monarch, was ordered to preach again on the next Sunday and apologize for the offense given. The day came, and with it a crowded assembly anxious to hear the bishop's apology. Reading his text, he commenced thus:

Hugh Latimer, dost thou know to whom thou art this day to speak? To the high and mighty monarch, the king's most excellent majesty, who can take away thy life if thou offendest; therefore, take heed that thou speakest not a word that may displease. But, then, consider well, Hugh Latimer, dost thou not know from *whence* thou comest, and upon *whose* message thou art sent? Even by the GREAT GOD, who is all-present and beholdeth all thy ways, who is omnipotent and able to cast both *body* and *soul* into hell together; therefore, take heed and deliver thy message faithfully.[1]

He then repeated the sermon of the previous Sunday, word for word, but with double its former energy and emphasis. The court was full of excitement to learn what would be the fate of this plain-dealing and fearless bishop. He was ordered into the king's presence, who, with a stern voice, asked, "How dared you thus offend me?" "I merely discharged my duty," was Latimer's reply. The king arose from his seat and embraced the good man, saying, "Blessed be God I have so honest a servant."

He was a worthy successor of Nathan, who confronted King David with his sin and said, "Thou art the man" (2 Sam. 12:7 KJV). This divine courage will surely accompany the fiery baptism of the Spirit. What is it but the indwelling of the Holy Spirit that gives courage to anointed preachers, enabling them to face danger and difficulty and loneliness with joy, and attack sin in its worst forms as fearlessly as David attacked Goliath?

"'Not by might nor by power, but by My Spirit,' says the LORD of hosts" (Zech. 4:6 NKJV).

Shall I, for fear of feeble man,
The Spirit's course in me restrain? . . .

Awed by a mortal's frown, shall I
Conceal the Word of God most high? . . .

Shall I, to soothe the unholy throng,
Soften Thy truth, or smooth my tongue? . . .

How then before Thee shall I dare
To stand, or how Thine anger bear? . . .

Yea, let men rage; since Thou wilt spread
Thy shadowing wings around my head;
Since in all pain Thy tender love
Will still my sure refreshment prove.[2]

He was without guile. Paul wrote to the Thessalonians, "You can see we were not preaching with any deceit or impure motives or trickery. For we speak as messengers approved by God to be entrusted with the Good News. Our purpose is to please God, not people. He alone examines the motives of our hearts" (1 Thess. 2:3–4 NLT).

Paul was frank and open. He spoke right out of his heart. He was transparently simple and straightforward. Since God had honored him with this infinite trust of preaching the gospel, he sought to so preach it that he would please God regardless of people's opinions. And yet that is the surest way to please people. People who listen to such preachers feel their honesty and realize that they are seeking to do them good, to save them rather than to tickle their ears and win their applause, and in their hearts they are pleased.

But whether or not people are pleased, anointed preachers deliver the message as ambassadors and look to their home government for their reward. They get their commission from God, and it is God who will try their hearts and prove their ministry. Oh, to please Jesus! Oh, to stand perfect before God after preaching His gospel!

He was not a time-server, nor a covetous man. Paul said, "Never once did we try to win you with flattery, as you well know. And God is our witness that we were not pretending to be your friends just to get your money!" (1 Thess. 2:5 NLT).

There are three ways of reaching someone's purse or wallet: (1) directly; (2) by way of the head with flattering words; or (3) by way of the heart with frank, honest, saving words. The first way is robbery. The second way is also robbery, with the poison of a deadly, but pleasing, opiate added, which may damn the hearer's soul. The third reaches the purse by saving the soul and opening in the heart an unfailing fountain of benevolence to bless the hearer and the world.

It would be better for a preacher to become a criminal and rob people with a club than to rob them with flattery, with smiles and smooth words and feigned and fawning affection, while their poor souls, neglected and deceived, go down to hell. How could anyone meet them in the day of judgment and look into their horror-stricken faces, realizing that he or she toyed with their fancies and affections and pride to get money and, instead of faithfully warning them and seeking to save them, with flattering words fattened their souls for destruction!

Not so did Paul. "I don't want what you have—I want you," he wrote the Corinthians (2 Cor. 12:14 NLT). It was not their money but their souls he wanted. But such faithful love will be able to command all others have to give. Why, to some of his newly minted Christians he wrote, "I am sure you would have taken out your own eyes and given them to me if it had been possible" (Gal. 4:15 NLT). But he sought not to please them with flattering words, only to save them.

Paul was so faithful in this matter, and so conscious of his integrity, that he called God Himself into the witness stand. "God is our witness," he said (1 Thess. 2:5 NLT). Blessed is anyone who can call on God to witness for him or her. And those in whom the Holy Spirit dwells in fullness can do this.

Paul was not vain, nor dictatorial, nor oppressive. Some people care nothing for money, but they care mightily for power and place and worldly glory. But Paul was free from this spiritual itch. Listen to him: "As for human praise, we have never sought it from you or anyone else" (1 Thess. 2:6 NLT).

Solomon said, "To seek one's own glory is not glory" (Prov. 25:27 NKJV), it is only vainglory. Jesus asked, "How can you believe since you accept glory from one another but do not seek the glory that comes from the only God?" (John 5:44 NIV).

Paul was free from all this, and so is everyone who is full of the Holy Spirit. And it is only as we are thus free that with the whole heart and with a single eye we can devote ourselves to the work of saving others.

With all his boldness and faithfulness, he was gentle. "We were gentle among you," Paul said, "just as a nursing mother cherishes her own children" (1 Thess. 2:7 NKJV). The fierce hurricane that casts down the giant trees of the forest is not so mighty as the gentle sunshine, which, from tiny seeds and acorns, lifts aloft the towering spires of oak and fir on a thousand hills and mountains.

The wild storm that lashes the sea into foam and fury is feeble compared to the gentle yet immeasurably powerful influence which twice a day swings the oceans in resistless tides from shore to shore. And as in the physical world the mighty powers are gentle in their vast workings, so it is in the spiritual world. The light that falls on the eyelids of the sleeping infant and wakes it from its slumber is not more gentle than the "still small voice" (1 Kings 19:12 KJV) that brings assurance of forgiveness or cleansing to them that look to Jesus.

Oh, the gentleness of God! "Your gentleness made me great," said David (Ps. 18:35 ESV). "By the humility and gentleness of Christ, I appeal to you," wrote Paul (2 Cor. 10:1 NIV). And again, "The fruit of the Spirit is love, joy, peace, longsuffering, gentleness" (Gal. 5:22 KJV). And as the Father, Son, and Holy Spirit are gentle, so will be the servant of the Lord who is filled with the Spirit.

I shall never forget the gentleness of a mighty man of God I knew, who on the platform was clothed with zeal as with a garment and in his overwhelming earnestness was like a lion or a consuming fire, but when dealing with a wounded or broken heart or with a seeking soul, no nurse with a little babe could be more tender than he.

Finally, Paul was full of self-forgetful, self-sacrificing love. Paul told the Thessalonians, "We loved you so much that we shared with you not only God's Good News but our own lives, too" (1 Thess. 2:8 NLT).

No wonder he shook those cities, overthrew their idols, and had great revivals! No wonder his jailer became a Christian and his churches would have gladly plucked out their eyes for him! Such tender, self-sacrificing love compels attention, begets confidence, enkindles love, and surely wins its object.

This burning love led him to labor and sacrifice and so live and walk before them that he was not only a teacher, but also an example of all he taught, and he could safely say, "Follow my example" (1 Cor. 11:1 NIV). This love led him to preach the whole truth that he might by all means save them. He kept back no truth because it was unpopular, for it was their salvation and not his own reputation and popularity he sought.

He did not preach himself, but a crucified Christ, without the shedding of whose blood there is no remission of sins. And through that precious blood he preached present cleansing from all sin and the gift of the Holy Spirit for all who obediently believe. And this love kept him faithful and humble and true to the end, so that at last in sight of the martyr's death, he saw the martyr's crown and cried out: "My life has already been poured out as an offering to God. . . . I have fought the good fight, I have finished the race, and I have remained faithful. And now the prize awaits me — the crown of righteousness, which the Lord, the righteous Judge, will give me on the day of his return" (2 Tim. 4:6–8 NLT).

Paul had been faithful, and at the end was oppressed with no doubts and harassed with no bitter regrets, but looked forward with eager joy to meeting his Lord and beholding the blessed face of Him he loved.

Have you received the Holy Ghost?
'Twill fit you for the fight,
'Twill make of you a mighty host,
To put your foes to flight.
Have you received the Holy Power?
'Twill fall from heaven on you,
From Jesus' throne this very hour,
'Twill make you brave and true.
Oh, now receive the Holy Fire!
'Twill burn away all dross,
All earthly, selfish, vain desire,
'Twill make you love the Cross.[3]

NOTES

1. William Suddards, *The British Pulpit: Consisting of Discourses by the Most Eminent Living Divines in England, Scotland, and Ireland* (Philadelphia: Grigg and Elliot; Desilver, Thomas and Company, 1837), 107.

2. Johann Joseph Winckler, "Shall I for Fear of Feeble Man," trans. John Wesley, 1739, public domain.

3. Author unknown, *Salvation Army Songs*, comp. William Booth (London: The Salvation Army Book Department, 1911), 339.

Preaching 17

"Where are the wise?" asked Paul. "Where are the legal experts? Where are today's debaters? Hasn't God made the wisdom of the world foolish?" And then he declared, "In God's wisdom, he determined that the world wouldn't come to know him through its wisdom. Instead, God was pleased to save those who believe through the foolishness of preaching" (1 Cor. 1:20–21 CEB).

What kind of preaching is this? He did not say, "foolish preaching," but the foolishness of such a thing as preaching. Certainly, it is not the moral essay, or the intellectual or semi-intellectual kind of preaching most generally heard throughout the world today that will change lives, for thousands of such sermons move and change no one. Nor is it a mere noisy declamation called a sermon—noisy because empty of all earnest thought and true feeling. But it must be the kind of which Peter spoke when he wrote of "those who preached in the power of the Holy Spirit sent from heaven" (1 Pet. 1:12 NLT).

No one is equipped to rightly preach the gospel and undertake the spiritual oversight and instruction of souls until he or she has been anointed with the Holy Spirit.

The disciples had been led to Jesus by John the Baptist, whose mighty preaching laid a deep and broad foundation for their spiritual education. Then for three years they had listened to both the public and private teachings of Jesus and had been "eyewitnesses of his majesty" (2 Pet. 1:16 KJV), of His life and death and resurrection, and yet He commanded them to remain in Jerusalem and wait for the Holy Spirit, who was to fit them for their ministry. And if they—trained and taught by the Master Himself—had need of the Holy Spirit to enable them to preach and testify with wisdom and power, how much more do you and I need His presence!

Without Him they could do nothing. With Him they were invincible and could continue Jesus' work. The mighty energy of His working is seen in Peter's preaching on the day of Pentecost. The sermon itself does not seem to have been very remarkable; indeed, it is principally composed of testimony backed up and fortified by Scripture quotations, followed by exhortation, as are the sermons that are most effective today in the immediate salvation and sanctification of souls. "True preaching," said Horace Bushnell, "is a testimony."[1]

Peter's Scripture quotations were apt, fitting the occasion and the people to whom they were addressed. The testimony was bold and joyous, the rushing outflow of a warm, fresh, throbbing experience. And the exhortation was burning, uncompromising in its demands, and yet tender and full of sympathy and love. But a divine Presence was at work in that vast, mocking, wondering throng, and it was He who made Peter's simple words search like fire and carry such overwhelming conviction to the hearts of the people.

And it is still so that whenever and wherever someone preaches "in the power of the Holy Spirit sent from heaven" (1 Pet. 1:12 NLT) there will be conviction.

Under Peter's sermon, "they were cut to the heart" (Acts 2:37 ESV). The truth pierced them as a sword until they said, "What shall we do?" They had been doubting and mocking a short time before, but now they were earnestly inquiring the way to be saved.

The speech may be without polish, the manner uncouth, and the matter simple and plain, but conviction will surely follow any preaching in the burning love and power and contagious joy of the Holy Spirit.

A few years ago, a poor young man in Africa, who had been stolen for a slave and most cruelly treated, heard a missionary talking of the indwelling of the Holy Spirit, and his heart hungered and thirsted for Him. In a strange manner, he worked his way to New York to find out more about the Holy Spirit, introducing the captain of the ship and several of the crew to Jesus Christ on the way. The brother in New York to whom he came took him to a meeting the first night he was in the city and left him there, while he went to fulfill another engagement. When he returned at a late hour, he found a crowd at the penitent form, led there by the simple words of this young man. He took him to his Sunday school and put him up to speak while he attended to some other matters. When he turned from these affairs that had occupied his attention for only a little while, he found the penitent form full of teachers and scholars, weeping before the Lord. What the young man had said he did not know, but he was bowed with wonder and filled with joy, for it was the power of the Holy Spirit.

The hearers of Wesley, Whitefield, Finney, and others used to fall as though cut down in battle under their preaching. And while there may not be the same physical manifestation at all times, there will surely be the same opening of eyes to spiritual things, breaking of hearts, and piercing of consciences. The Holy Spirit will often come upon a congregation like a wind under the preaching of someone filled with the Spirit, and heads will droop, eyes will brim with tears, and hearts will break under His convicting power. I remember a proud young woman, who had been mercilessly criticizing us for several nights, smitten in this way. She was smiling when suddenly the Holy Spirit winged a word to her heart and instantly her countenance changed. Her head drooped and for an hour or more she sobbed and struggled while her proud heart broke, and she found her way with true repentance and faith to the feet of Jesus and her heavenly Father's favor. How often have we seen such sights as this under the preaching of General William Booth! And it ought to be a common sight under the preaching of all servants of God, for what are we sent for but to convict people of their sin and their need, and by the power of the Spirit to lead them to the Savior? And not only will there be conviction under such preaching, but generally, if not always, there will be salvation and sanctification.

Three thousand people accepted Christ after Peter's Pentecostal sermon. Later five thousand were added to the kingdom, and a multitude of the priests were obedient to the faith. And it was so under the preaching of Philip in Samaria, of Peter in Lydda and Saron and Caesarea, and of Paul in Ephesus and other cities.

To be sure, Stephen's preaching, in its immediate effect, only resulted in enraging his hearers until they stoned him to death. But it is highly probable that the ultimate result was the conversion of Paul, who held the clothes of those who stoned Stephen. And through Paul came the evangelization of the Gentiles.

One of the greatest of American evangelists sought the baptism with the Holy Spirit with agonizing prayers and tears, and received it. And then, he said, he preached the same sermons, but where before it had been as one beating the air, now hundreds experienced new life through faith in Jesus Christ.

It is this that has made Salvation Army officers (ministers) successful. Young, inexperienced, without special gifts and without learning, but with the baptism, they have been mighty to win souls. The hardest hearts have been broken, the darkest minds illuminated, the most stubborn wills subdued, and the wildest natures tamed by them. Their words have been "with power" (Luke 4:32 KJV) and have convicted and saved and sanctified souls, and whole communities have been transformed by their labors.

But without this Presence, great gifts and profound and accurate learning are without avail in the salvation of souls. We often see people with great natural powers, splendidly trained, and equipped with everything save this fiery baptism, and they labor and preach year after year without seeing a soul enter God's kingdom. They have spent years in study but they have not spent a day (much less ten days) fasting and praying and waiting upon God for His anointing that would fill them with heavenly wisdom and power for their work. They are like a great gun loaded and primed, but without a spark of fire to turn the powder and ball into an irresistible lightning bolt.

It is fire we need, and we get it from God in agonizing, wrestling, listening prayer that will not be denied. And when we get it, and not until then, will we preach with the Holy Spirit sent down from heaven, and surely souls will be saved. Such preaching is not foolish. On the contrary:

Preaching in the power of the Holy Spirit is reasonable. It takes account of human reason and conforms to the dictates of common sense. We read that Paul reasoned with the people in the synagogues (see Acts 17:2; 18:4, 19). His preaching was not a noisy harangue nor a rose-water essay of pretty, empty platitudes, but a life and death—eternal life and death—grapple with the intelligence of his listeners. God is the Author of our intellectual powers, and He endowed Paul with reason. The Holy Spirit respects these powers and appeals to reason when He inspires men and women to preach.

Preaching in the power of the Holy Spirit is persuasive. "Come now, let us reason together, says the LORD" (Isa. 1:18 ESV). He takes account of people's feelings, sensibilities, fears, hopes, and affections, and persuades them. Human beings are not all intellect, a mere logic machine. They are a bundle of sensibilities as well. And true preaching—the kind that is inspired by the Holy Spirit—appeals to the whole person. It appeals to the intelligence with reasons and arguments, but is also penetrated through and through with such a spirit of compassionate persuasiveness that wholesome fears are aroused, shame of sin is created, conscience is unshackled, desires for purity and goodness are resurrected, tender affections are quickened, the will is energized, and the whole person is fired and illuminated by a flame of saving emotions, kindled by the fire in the preacher's heart. And this flame enables the hearer to see and feel the realities of things eternal, of God and judgment, of heaven and hell, of the final fixedness of moral character, and of the importance of immediate repentance and acceptance of God's offer of mercy in Jesus Christ.

Preaching in the power of the Holy Spirit is scriptural. The gospel is not opposed to natural religion and reason but it has run far ahead of them. It is a revelation from God of facts, of grace and truth, of mercy and love, and of a plan of redemption that humans could not discover for themselves. And this revelation is recorded in the Scriptures. So we find that Paul "reasoned with them out of the scriptures" (Acts 17:2 KJV). The truths of the Bible cover people's moral needs as a glove covers a hand, fits their moral nature and experience as a key fits its lock, and reveals the condition of their heart as a mirror reveals the state of a face.

No one can read the Bible thoughtfully without either hating it or hating his or her own sins. But while it reveals our sin and our lost condition, it also declares God's love and His plan of redemption. It shows us Jesus Christ, the way by which we come to Him, and how through Him we get deliverance from sin and become a new creation. It is in the Bible, and only there, that this revelation can be found. And that is what the Holy Spirit inspires men and women to preach.

"We preach Christ crucified," wrote Paul (1 Cor. 1:23 KJV). And again, "We preach not ourselves, but Christ Jesus the Lord" (2 Cor. 4:5 KJV). And he exhorted Timothy to "preach the word" (2 Tim. 4:2 KJV).

It is the unsearchable but revealed "riches of Christ" that we are to preach (Eph. 3:8 KJV).

The Holy Spirit makes the Word alive. He brings it to the remembrance of the preachers in whom He abides, and He applies it to the heart of the hearers, lightening up the soul as with a sun until sin is seen in all its hideousness, or cutting as a sharp sword, piercing the heart with irresistible conviction of the guilt and shame of sin.

Peter had no time to consult the Scriptures and prepare a sermon on the morning of Pentecost. But the Holy Spirit quickened his memory and brought to his mind the Scriptures appropriate to the occasion.

Hundreds of years before, the Holy Spirit, by the mouth of the prophet Joel, had foretold that in the last days the Spirit would be poured out upon all flesh and their sons and daughters would prophesy. And the same Spirit that spoke through Joel now made Peter see and declare that this Pentecostal baptism was that of which Joel spoke.

By the mouth of David, He had said, "You will not leave my soul among the dead or allow your holy one to rot in the grave" (Ps. 16:10 NLT), and now Peter, by the inspiration of the same Spirit, applied this Scripture to the resurrection of Jesus, and so proved to his fellow Jews that the One they had condemned and killed was the Holy One foretold in prophecy and psalm.

And so today the Holy Spirit inspires those who receive Him to use the Scriptures to awaken, convict, and save souls.

When Finney was a young preacher, he was invited to a country schoolhouse to preach. On the way there, he became much distressed in soul, and his mind seemed blank and dark, when all at once this text, spoken to Lot in Sodom by the angels, came to his mind: "Up, get you out of this place; for the LORD will destroy this city" (Gen. 19:14 KJV). He explained the text, told the people about Lot and the wickedness of Sodom, and applied it to them. While he spoke, they began to look exceedingly angry, and then, as he earnestly exhorted them to give up their sins and seek the Lord, they began to fall from their seats as though stricken down in battle and cried to God for mercy. A great revival followed. Many came to faith in Christ, and a number of those became ministers of the gospel.

To Finney's amazement, he learned afterward that the place was called Sodom because of its extreme wickedness, and the old man who had invited him to preach was called Lot, because he was the only God-fearing man in the place. Evidently the Holy Spirit worked through Finney to accomplish these results. And such inspiration is not uncommon with those who are filled with the Spirit.

But this reinforcement of the mind and memory by the Holy Spirit does not do away with the need of study. The Spirit quickens that which is already in the mind and memory, as the warm sun and rains of spring quicken the sleeping seeds that are in the ground, and only those. The sun does not put the seed in the soil, nor does the Holy Spirit without our attention and study put the Word of God in our minds. For that we should prayerfully and patiently study.

The apostles of Jesus said, "We will give ourselves continually to prayer, and to the ministry of the word" (Acts 6:4 KJV). And Paul wrote to Timothy, "Be diligent to present yourself approved to God, a worker who does not need to be ashamed, rightly dividing the word of truth" (2 Tim. 2:15 NKJV).

Those who have most carefully and prayerfully studied the Word of God, and most constantly and lovingly meditated upon it, have been best able to rightly divide the Word, and have been most mightily used by the Holy Spirit.

Preaching in the power of the Holy Spirit is healing and comforting. It is indescribably searching in its effects. But it is also edifying, strengthening, and comforting to those who are wholly the Lord's. It cuts, but only to cure. It searches, but only to save. It is constructive as well as destructive. It tears down sin and pride and unbelief, but it builds up faith and righteousness and holiness and all the graces of a Christian character. It warms the heart with love, strengthens faith, and confirms the will in all holy purposes.

Every preacher baptized with the Holy Spirit can say with Jesus, "The Spirit of the LORD is upon me, for he has anointed me to bring Good News to the poor. He has sent me to proclaim that captives will be released, that the blind will see, that the oppressed will be set free, and that the time of the LORD's favor has come" (Luke 4:18–19 NLT).

Seldom is there a congregation in which there are only those who need to be convicted. There will also be meek and gentle ones to whom should be brought a message of joy and good tidings, brokenhearted ones to be bound up, wounded ones to be healed, tempted ones to be delivered, and those whom Satan has bound by some fear or habit to be set free. And the Holy Spirit who knows all hearts will inspire the word that shall bless these needy ones.

The preacher filled with the Holy Spirit, who is instant in prayer, constant in the study of God's Word, and steadfast and active in faith, will surely be so helped that he or she can say with Isaiah, "The Sovereign

LORD has given me his words of wisdom, so that I know how to comfort the weary" (Isa. 50:4 NLT). And as with little Samuel, the Lord will "let none of his words fall to the ground" (1 Sam. 3:19 KJV). Such a preacher will expect results, and God will make them follow his or her preaching as surely as corn follows the planting and cultivating of the farmer.

NOTE

1. Horace Bushnell, *Nature and the Supernatural Together Constituting the One System of God* (New York: Charles Scribner, 1858), 515.

The Holy Spirit's Call 18

The testimony of the worker God is this: "The Spirit of the Sovereign LORD is upon me, for the LORD has anointed me to bring good news to the poor" (Isa. 61:1 NLT). God chooses His own coworkers, and it is the office of the Holy Spirit to call whom He will to preach the gospel. I do not doubt that He calls people to other employments for His glory, and would still more often do so, if people would just listen and wait upon Him to know His will.

He called Bezaleel and Aholiab to build the tabernacle. He called and commissioned the Gentile king, Cyrus, to rebuild Jerusalem and restore His chastised and humbled people to their own land. And did He not call Joan of Arc to her strange and wonderful mission? And Washington and Lincoln?

And, no doubt, He leads most men and women by His providence to their lifework. But the call to preach the gospel is more than a providential leading; it is a distinct and imperative conviction. Methodist bishop Matthew Simpson, in his *Lectures on Preaching*, said:

Even in its faintest form there is this distinction between the call to the ministry and the choice of other professions: The young man may *wish* to be a physician; he may *desire* to enter the navy; he *would like* to be a farmer; but he feels he *ought* to be a minister; and it is this feeling of "ought" and obligation which in its feeblest form indicates the divine call. It is not in the aptitude, taste, or desire, but in the *conscience* that its root is found. It is God's voice to the man's conscience, saying: "You *ought* to preach."[1]

Sometimes the call comes as distinctly as though a voice had spoken from the skies into the depths of the heart.

A young man who was studying law experienced new life in Christ. After a while, he was convicted for sanctification and while seeking heard a voice saying, "Will you devote all your time to the Lord?" He replied, "I am to be a lawyer, not a preacher, Lord." But not until he had said, "Yes, Lord," could he find the blessing.

A thoughtless, godless young fellow was working in the cornfield when a telegram was handed to him announcing the death of his brother, a brilliant and devoted Salvation Army officer (pastor). There and then, unsaved as he was, God called him, showed him a vast Army with ranks broken, where his brother had fallen, and made him to feel that he should fill the breach in the ranks. Fourteen months later he took up the sword and entered the fight from the same platform from which his brother fell, and is today one of our most successful and promising officers.

Again, the call may come as a quiet suggestion, a gentle conviction, as though a gossamer bridle were placed upon the heart and conscience to guide that person into the work of the Lord. The suggestion gradually becomes clearer. The conviction strengthens until it masters the one who is called, and if that person seeks to escape it, he or she finds the silken bridle to be one of stoutest thongs and firmest steel.

It was so with me. When I was just a boy of eleven, I heard a man preaching, and I said to myself, "Oh, how beautiful to preach!" Two years later I became a Christian, and soon the conviction came upon me that I should preach. Later, I decided to follow another profession but the conviction to preach increased in strength, while I struggled against it and turned away my ears and went on with my studies. Yet in every crisis or hour of stillness, when my soul faced God, the conviction that I must preach burned itself deeper into my conscience. I rebelled against it. I felt I would almost rather (but not quite) go to hell than to submit. Then at last a great "Woe is me if I do not preach the gospel" (1 Cor. 9:16 NKJV) took possession of me, and I yielded, and God won.

The first year He gave me three revivals, with many souls. And now I would rather preach Jesus to skeptics and seekers and feed His lambs than be an archangel before the throne. Someday He will call me into His blessed presence and I shall stand before His face and praise Him forever for counting me worthy and calling me to preach His glad gospel and share in His joy of saving the lost. The "woe" is lost in love and delight through the baptism of the Spirit and the sweet assurance that Jesus is pleased.

Occasionally, the call comes to someone who is ready and responds promptly and gladly. When Isaiah received the fiery touch that purged his life and purified his heart, he "heard the voice of the Lord, saying, 'Whom shall I send, and who will go for us?'" And in the joy and power of his new experience, he cried out, "Here am I; send me." (Isa. 6:8 KJV).

When Paul received his call, he said, "I did not rush out to consult with any human being" (Gal. 1:16 NLT) but got up and went as the Lord led him.

But more often it seems the Lord finds people preoccupied with other plans and ambitions, or encompassed with obstacles and difficulties, or oppressed with a deep sense of unworthiness or unfitness. Moses argued that he could not talk. He said, "O Lord, I'm not very good with words. I never have been, and I'm not now, even though you have spoken to me. I get tongue-tied, and my words get tangled" (Ex. 4:10 NLT).

And then the Lord condescended, as He always does, to reason with the backward man: "Who makes a person's mouth? Who decides whether people speak or do not speak, hear or do not hear, see or do not see? Is it not I, the LORD? Now go! I will be with you as you speak, and I will instruct you in what to say" (Ex. 4:11–12 NLT).

When the call of God came to Jeremiah, he shrank back, and said, "O Sovereign LORD . . . I can't speak for you! I'm too young!' But the Lord said in response, "Don't say, 'I'm too young,' for you must go wherever I send you and say whatever I tell you. And don't be afraid of the people, for I will be with you and will protect you. I, the LORD, have spoken!" (Jer. 1:6–8 NLT). And so the call of God comes today to those who shrink and feel that they are the most unfit or most hedged in by insuperable difficulties.

I know a man who, when he became a Christian, could not tell A from B. He knew nothing whatever about the Bible and stammered so badly that, when asked his own name, it would usually take him a minute or so to tell it. Added to this, he lisped badly and was subject to a nervous affliction which seemed likely to unfit him for any kind of work whatever. But God poured light and love into his heart, called him to preach, and today he is one of the mightiest soul-winners in the whole round of my acquaintance. When he speaks, the house is always packed to the doors and the people hang on his words with wonder and joy.

He entered God's kingdom at a camp meeting and was sanctified wholly in a cornfield. He learned to read, but—being too poor to afford a light in the evening—he studied a large-print Bible by the light of the full moon. Today, he has the Bible almost committed to memory, and when he speaks he does not open the Book but reads his lesson from memory, quotes proof texts from Genesis to Revelation without mistake, and gives chapter and verse for every quotation. When he talks, his face shines, and his speech is like honey for sweetness and like bullets fired from a gun for power. He is one of the weak and foolish ones God has chosen to confound the wise and mighty (see 1 Cor. 1:27).

If God calls you, He will so corroborate the call in some way that others will know there is a prophet among them. It will be with you as it was with Samuel: "And Samuel grew, and the LORD was with him, and did let none of his words fall to the ground. And all Israel from Dan even to Beersheba knew that Samuel was established to be a prophet of the LORD" (1 Sam. 3:19–20 KJV).

If you are uncertain about the call, God will deal patiently with you, as He did with Gideon, to make you certain. Your fleece will be wet with dew when the earth is dry, or dry when the earth is wet. Or you will hear of some tumbling barley cake smiting the tents of Midian, that will strengthen your faith and make you know that God is with you (see Judg. 6:36–40; 7:9–15).

If the door is shut and difficulties hedge the way, God will go before the one He calls, open the door, and sweep away the difficulties (see Isa. 45:2–3).

If others think you so ignorant and unfit that they doubt your call, God will give you such grace or such power to win souls that they shall have to acknowledge that God has chosen you. It was in this way that God made a whole Salvation Army national headquarters, from the top down, to know that He had chosen the elevator operator for His work. The young man got scores of his passengers on the elevator saved, and then he was commissioned and sent into the field to devote all his time to saving souls.

The Lord will surely let your brothers and sisters know, as surely as He did the church at Antioch, when "the Holy Spirit said, 'Dedicate Barnabas and Saul for the special work to which I have called them'" (Acts 13:2 NLT).

Sometimes the one who is called will try to hide it in his or her heart, and then God stirs up someone to lay a hand on a shoulder, and ask, "Are you not called to the work?" And the called one finds it impossible to hide or escape from the call, no more than Adam could hide himself from God behind the trees of the garden or Jonah escape God's call by taking a ship for Tarshish.

Happy are they who do not try to escape but, though trembling at the mighty responsibility, assume it and with all humility and faithfulness set to work by prayer and patient, continuous study of God's Word to fit themselves for God's work. They will need to prepare themselves, for the call to the work is also a call to preparation, continuous preparation of the fullest possible kind.

Those whom God calls cannot safely neglect or despise the call. They will find their mission on earth, their happiness and peace, their power and prosperity, their reward in heaven, and probably heaven itself, bound up with that call and dependent upon it. They may run away from it, as Jonah did, and find a waiting ship to favor their flight, but they will also find fierce storms and bellowing seas overtaking them, and big-mouthed fishes of trouble and disaster ready to swallow them.

But if they heed the call and cheerfully go where God appoints, God will go with them; they shall nevermore be left alone. The Holy Spirit will surely accompany them, and they may be among the happiest souls on earth, one of the gladdest creatures in God's universe.

"Be sure of this: I am with you always, even to the end of the age" (Matt. 28:20 NLT), said Jesus as He commissioned His disciples to go to all nations and preach the gospel. "I will personally go with you" (Ex. 33:14 NLT), said Jehovah to Moses, when sending him to face Pharaoh, free Israel, and lead them to the Promised Land.

And to the boy Jeremiah, He said, "Don't be afraid of the people, for I will be with you and will protect you. . . . They will fight you, but they will fail. For I am with you" (Jer. 1:8, 19 NLT).

I used to read these words with a great and rapturous joy as I realized by faith that they were also meant for me, and for everyone sent of God, and that His blessed presence was with me every time I spoke to the people or dealt with an individual soul or knelt in prayer with a penitent seeker after God. And I still read them so.

Has He called you? Are you conscious of His helpful, sympathizing, loving presence with you? If so, let no petty offense, hardship, danger, or dread of the future, cause you to turn aside or draw back. Stick to the work till He calls you out, and when He so calls you can go with open face and a heart abounding with love, joy, and peace, and He will still go with you.

NOTE

1. Matthew Simpson, *Lectures on Preaching* (London: Richard D. Dickinson, 1879), 25.

The Sheathed Sword: A Law of the Spirit 19

Just as the moss and the oak are higher in the order of creation than the clod of clay and the rock, the bird and beast higher than the moss and the oak, the human than the bird and the beast, so the spiritual being is higher than the natural being. The sons and daughters of God are a new order of being. The Christian is a "new creation" (2 Cor. 5:17 ESV).

Just as there are laws governing the life of the plant, and other and higher laws that apply to the bird and beast, so there are higher laws for human beings, and still higher for the Christian. It was with regard to one of these higher laws that govern the heavenly life of the Christian that Jesus said to Peter, "Put away your sword" (Matt. 26:52 NLT).

Jesus said to Pilate, "My Kingdom is not an earthly kingdom. If it were, my followers would fight" (John 18:36 NLT). The unspiritual person's kingdom is of this world, and it is the law of the carnal nature to fight with fist and sword, tongue and wit. Therefore, that person will fight for it with such weapons as this world furnishes.

Christians, however, are citizens of heaven, and they are subject to its law, which is universal, wholehearted love. In this kingdom, we conquer not by fighting but by submitting. When an enemy takes my coat, I overcome him not by going to the law but by generously giving him my cloak also. When my enemy compels me to go a mile with him, I vanquish the enemy by cheerfully going two miles with him. When I am smitten on one cheek, I win my foe by meekly turning the other cheek. This is the law of the new life from heaven, and only by recognizing and obeying it can that new life be sustained and passed on to others. This is the narrow way that leads to life eternal, and few find it (see Matt. 7:14) or, finding it, are willing to walk in it.

A Russian peasant named Sutajeff could get no help from the religious teachers of his village, so he learned to read, and while studying the Bible he found this narrow way and walked gladly in it. One night neighbors of his stole some of his grain, but in their haste or carelessness they left a bag. He found it and ran after them to restore it. "For," said he, "fellows who have to steal must be hard up." And by this Christlike spirit he saved both himself and them, for he kept the spirit of love in his own heart, and they were won to the faith and became his most ardent disciples.

On another occasion, a beggar woman to whom he gave lodging stole the bedding and ran away with it. She was pursued by the neighbors and was just about to be put in prison when Sutajeff appeared, became her advocate, secured her acquittal, and gave her food and money for her journey. He recognized the law of his new life and gladly obeyed it, and so was not overcome by evil, but persistently and triumphantly overcame evil with good (see Rom. 12:21).

This is the spirit and method of Jesus. He came not to be ministered unto, but to minister and to give His life a ransom for many. And by those who are filled with this spirit and following this method He will yet win the world. His spirit is not one of self-seeking but of self-sacrifice. Some mysterious majesty of His presence or voice so awed and overcame His foes that they stepped back and fell to the ground before Him in the garden of His agony, but He meekly submitted Himself to them. And when Peter drew his sword and cut off the ear of the high priest's servant, Jesus said to him, "Put your sword back into its sheath. Shall I not drink from the cup of suffering the Father has given me?" (John 18:11 NLT).

This was the spirit of Isaac. When he dug a well, the Philistines disputed with his servants for it. So he dug another. And when they claimed that, he removed and dug yet another. "This time there was no dispute over it, so Isaac named the place Rehoboth (which means 'open space'), for he said, 'At last the LORD has created enough space for us to prosper in this land' . . . [And] the LORD appeared to him on the night of his arrival. 'I am the God of your father, Abraham,' he said. 'Do not be afraid, for I am with you and will bless you. I will multiply your descendants, and they will become a great nation'" (Gen. 26:22, 24 NLT).

This was the spirit of David when Saul was hunting for his life. Twice David could have slain him, and when urged to do so, he said, "Surely the LORD will strike Saul down someday, or he will die of old age or in battle. The LORD forbid that I should kill the one he has anointed!" (1 Sam. 26:10–11 NLT).

This was the spirit of Paul. He said, "We bless those who curse us. We are patient with those who abuse us. We appeal gently when evil things are said about us" (1 Cor. 4:12–13 NLT). "A servant of the Lord must not quarrel," wrote Paul to Timothy, "but must be kind to everyone" (2 Tim. 2:24 NLT). This is the spirit of our King. This is the law of His kingdom.

Is this your spirit? When you are reviled, demeaned, and slandered, and are tempted to retort, Jesus says to you, "Put away your sword" (Matt. 26:52 NLT). When you are wronged and ill-treated, and people ride roughshod over you, and you feel it would be simple justice to smite back, He says, "Put away your sword" and, "Live in peace with everyone" (Rom. 12:18 NLT). Your weapons are not carnal but spiritual now that you belong to Him and have your citizenship in heaven. If you fight with the sword, if you retort and strike back when you are wronged, you quench the Spirit—you get out of the narrow way, and your new life from heaven will perish.

A Salvation Army officer went to a hard corps (church) and found that his predecessor was sending back to friends, asking for money. The successor, losing sight of the spirit of Jesus, made a complaint about it, and the money was returned. But he became lean in his soul. He had quenched the spirit. He had broken the law of the kingdom. He had not only refused to give his cloak, but had also fought for and secured the return of the coat. He had lost the smile of Jesus, and his poor heart was sad and heavy within him. He came to me with anxious inquiry as to what I thought of his action. I had to admit that the other man had transgressed and that the money ought to be returned. But I felt that the officer should have been more grieved over the un-Christlike spirit of his brother than over the loss of the money, and that like Sutajeff, the Russian peasant, he should have said, "Poor fellow! He must be hard up; I will send him money myself." When I told him that story, he came to himself very quickly and was soon back in the narrow way and rejoicing in the smile of Jesus once again.

"But," you ask, "will not people walk over us if we do not stand up for our rights?" I do not argue that you are not to stand up for your rights but that you are to stand up for your higher rather than your lower rights, the rights of your heavenly life rather than your earthly life, and that you are to stand up for your rights in the way and spirit of Jesus rather than in the way and spirit of the world.

If others wrong you intentionally, they wrong themselves far worse than they wrong you. And if you have the spirit of Jesus in your heart, you will pity them more than you pity yourself. They nailed Jesus to the cross and hung Him up to die. They gave Him gall and vinegar to drink. They cast votes for His seamless robe and divided His garments between them while the crowd wagged their heads at Him and mocked Him. Great was the injustice and wrong they were inflicting upon Him, but He was not filled with anger, only pity. He thought not of the wrong done Him, but of the wrong they did themselves, and their sin against His heavenly Father. And He prayed not for judgment upon them, but that they might be forgiven, and He won them, and is winning and will win the world.

"By mercy and truth iniquity is purged," wrote Solomon (Prov. 16:6 KJV). "Put away your sword" and take mercy and truth for your weapons, and God will be with you and for you. And great shall be your victory and joy.

Victory over Suffering 20

Had there been no sin, our heavenly Father would have found other means by which to develop passive virtues in us and train us in the graces of meekness, patience, longsuffering, and forbearance, which so beautify and display the Christian character. But since sin is here—with its contradictions and falsehoods, its darkness, wars, brutalities, and injustices, producing awful harvests of pain and sorrow—God, in wonderful wisdom and loving-kindness, turns even these into instruments by which to fashion beautiful graces in us. Storm succeeds sunshine, and darkness the light. Pain follows hard on the heels of pleasure, while sorrow peers over the shoulder of joy. Gladness and grief, rest and toil, peace and war, interminably intermingled, follow each other in ceaseless succession in this world. We cannot escape suffering while in the body. But we can receive it with a faith that robs it of its terror and extracts from it richest blessing; from the flinty rock will gush forth living waters, and the carcass of the lion will furnish the sweetest honey.

This is so even when the suffering is a result of our own folly or sin. It is intended not only in some measure as a punishment, but also as a teacher, a corrective, a remedy, a warning. And it will surely work for good if, instead of repining and vainly regretting the past, we steadily look to Jesus and learn our lesson in patience and thankfulness.

If all the skies were sunshine,
Our faces would be fain
To feel once more upon them
The cooling plash of rain.
If all the world were music,
Our hearts would often long
For one sweet strain of silence
To break the endless song.
If life were always merry,
Our souls would seek relief
And rest from weary laughter
In the quiet arms of grief.[1]

Doubtless all our suffering is a result of sin, but not necessarily the sin of the sufferer. Jesus was the sinless One, but He was also the Chief of sufferers. Paul's great and lifelong sufferings came upon him not because of his sins but rather because he had forsaken sin and was following Jesus in a world of sin and seeking the salvation of others. In this path there is no escape from suffering, though there are hidden and inexpressible consolations. "In the world you will have tribulation," said Jesus (John 16:33 ESV). "Everyone who wants to live a godly life in Christ Jesus will suffer persecution," wrote Paul (2 Tim. 3:12 NLT).

Sooner or later, suffering in some form comes to each of us. It may come through broken health; or through pain and weariness of body; or through mental anguish, moral distress, spiritual darkness, and uncertainty. It may come through the loss of loved ones, betrayal by trusted friends, deferred or ruined hopes, or base ingratitude. It may come in unrequited toil and sacrifice and unfulfilled ambitions. But nothing more clearly distinguishes the person filled with the Spirit from one who is not than the way each receives suffering.

One person, with triumphant faith and shining face and strong heart glories in tribulation counts it all joy. To this class belong the apostles, who, beaten and threatened, "departed from the presence of the council, rejoicing that they were counted worthy to suffer shame for his name" (Acts 5:41 KJV). The other responds with doubts and fears, murmurs and complaints, and to other miseries adds that of a rebellious heart and discontented mind.

One sees the Enemy's armed host and unmixed distress and danger; the other sees the angel of the Lord, with abundant help and safety (see 2 Kings 6:15–17). A pastor went one morning to visit two women who were greatly afflicted. They were about the same age and had long been professing Christians and members of the church. He asked the first one upon whom he called, "How is it with you this morning?"

"Oh, I have not slept all night," she replied. "I have so much pain. It is so hard to have to lie here. I cannot see why God deals so with me."

Evidently, she was not filled with the Spirit but was in a controversy with the Lord about her sufferings and would not be comforted.

Leaving her, he called immediately upon the other woman and asked, "How are you today?"

"Oh, I had such a night of suffering!" she replied. Then, there broke upon her worn face, furrowed and pale, a beautiful radiance, and she added, "but Jesus was so near and helped me so, that I could suffer this way and more, if my Father thinks best." On she went with similar words of cheer and triumph that made the sick room a vestibule of glory. No lack of comfort in her heart, for the Comforter Himself, the Holy Spirit, had been invited and had come in. One had the Comforter in fullness, the other had not.

Probably no one ever suffered more than Paul, but with soldier-like fortitude he bore his heavy burdens; faced his constant and exacting labors; and endured his sore trials, disappointments, and bitter persecutions by fierce and relentless enemies. He stood unmoved amid shipwrecks, stripes, imprisonments, cold, hunger, and homelessness without a whimper that might suggest repining or discouragement or an appeal for pity. Indeed, he went beyond simple uncomplaining fortitude, and said, "We glory in tribulations" (Rom. 5:3 KJV), "I am exceeding joyful in all our tribulation" (2 Cor. 7:4 KJV), and "I take pleasure in infirmities, in reproaches, in necessities, in persecutions, in distresses for Christ's sake" (2 Cor. 12:10 KJV). After a terrible scourging upon his bare back, he was thrust into a loathsome inner dungeon, his feet fast in the stocks, with worse things probably awaiting him on the morrow. Nevertheless, we find him and Silas, his companion in suffering, at midnight praying and singing praises to God (see Acts 16:25).

What was his secret? Listen to him: "Because God's love has been poured into our hearts through the Holy Spirit who has been given to us" (Rom. 5:5 ESV). His prayer for his Ephesian brothers and sisters had been answered in his own heart: "That from his glorious, unlimited resources he will empower you with inner strength through his Spirit. Then Christ will make his home in your hearts" (Eph. 3:16–17 NLT). And this inner strength and consciousness, through faith in an indwelling Christ, enabled Paul to receive suffering and trial, not stoically, nor hilariously, in a spirit of bravado, but cheerfully and with a thankful heart.

Dr. Thomas Arnold, headmaster of Rugby School, wrote something about a "most dear and blessed sister" that illustrates the power flowing from exhaustless fountains of inner joy and strength through the working of the Holy Spirit. He said:

> I never saw a more perfect instance of the spirit and power of love and of a sound mind . . . a daily martyrdom for twenty years, during which she adhered to her early formed resolution of never talking about herself—enjoying everything lovely, graceful, beautiful, high-minded, whether in God's work or man's, with the keenest relish; inheriting the earth to the very fullness of the promise; and preserved through the very valley of the shadow of death from all fear or impatience, or from every cloud of impaired reason which might mar the beauty of Christ's glorious work.[2]

It is not by hypnotizing the soul, nor by blessing it into a state of ecstatic insensibility, that the Lord enables the person filled with the

Spirit to thus triumph over suffering. Rather it is by giving the soul a sweet, constant, and unshaken assurance through faith: First, that it is freely and fully accepted in Christ.

Second, that whatever suffering comes, it is measured, weighed, and permitted by love infinitely tender, and is guided by wisdom that cannot err.

Third, that however difficult it may be to explain suffering now, it is nevertheless one of the "all things" which "work together for good to them that love God" (Rom. 8:28 KJV) and that in a "little while" it will not only be swallowed up in ineffable blessedness and glory, but that in some way it is actually helping to work out "a far more exceeding and eternal weight of glory" (2 Cor. 4:17 KJV).

Fourth, that though the furnace has been heated seven times hotter than usual, yet "the form . . . like the Son of God" is walking with us in the fire (Dan. 3:25 KJV); though triumphant enemies have thrust us into the lions' den, yet the angel of the Lord arrived first and locked the lions' jaws; though foes may have formed sharp weapons against us, yet they cannot prosper, for His shield and buckler defend us; though all things be lost, yet "you remain forever" (Heb. 1:11 NLT); and though "my health may fail, and my spirit may grow weak . . . God remains the strength of my heart; he is mine forever" (Ps. 73:26 NLT).

Not all God's dear children thus triumph over their difficulties and sufferings, but this is God's standard, and they may attain to it if, by faith, they will open their hearts and "be filled with the Holy Spirit" (Eph. 5:18 NLT).

Here is the testimony of a Salvation Army officer:

Viewed from the outside, my life as a sinner was easy and untroubled, over which most of my friends expressed envy; while these same friends thought my life as a Christian full of care, toil, hardship, and immense loss. This, however, was only an outside view, and the real state of the case was exactly the opposite of what they supposed. For in all the pleasure-seeking, idleness, and freedom from responsibility of my life apart from God, I carried an immeasurable burden of fear, anxiety, and constantly recurring disappointment; trifles weighed upon me, and the thought of death haunted me with vague terrors.

But when I gave myself wholly to God, though my lot became at once one of toil, responsibility, comparative poverty, and sacrifice, yet I could not feel pain in any storm that broke over my head, because of the presence of God. It was not so much that I was insensible to trouble, as sensible of His presence and love; and the worst trials were as nothing in my sight, nor have been for over twenty-two years. While as for death, it appears only as a doorway into more abundant life, and I can alter an old German hymn, and sing with joy:

Oh, how my heart with rapture dances.

To think my dying hour advances!

Then, Lord, with Thee!

My Lord, with Thee!

This is faith's triumph over the worst the world can offer through the blessed fullness of the indwelling Comforter.

Here speaks the Comforter, Light of the straying,

Hope of the penitent, Advocate sure,

Joy of the desolate, tenderly saying,

Earth has no sorrow that heaven cannot cure.[3]

NOTES

1. Henry Van Dyke, "If All the Skies," *Songs Out of Doors* (New York: Charles Scribner's Sons, 1922), 39.

2. Robert Gracey Ferguson, *Baccalaureate Sermons* (Boston: Richard G. Badger, The Gorham Press, 1919), 75.

3. Thomas Moore, "Come, Ye Disconsolate," 1816, public domain.

The Overflowing Blessing 21

Moses instructed the children of Israel to give tithes of all they had to the Lord, and in return God promised to richly bless them, making their fields and vineyards fruitful and causing their flocks and herds to safely multiply. But they became covetous and unbelieving, and began to rob God by withholding their tithes, and then God began to withhold His blessing from them.

But still God loved and pitied them, and spoke to them again and again by His prophets. Finally, by the prophet Malachi, He said, 'Bring all the tithes into the storehouse so there will be enough food in my Temple. If you do,' says the Lord of Heaven's Armies, 'I will open the windows of heaven for you. I will pour out a blessing so great you won't have enough room to take it in! Try it! Put me to the test!' (Mal. 3:10 NLT). He promised to make their barns overflow if they would be faithful, if they would pay their tithes and discharge their obligations to Him.

Now, this overflow of barns and granaries is a picture of how our hearts and lives overflow when we give ourselves fully to God, the blessed Holy Spirit comes in, and Jesus becomes all and in all to us. The blessing is too big to contain, but just bursts out and overflows through the life, the looks, the conversation, and the very tones of the voice, and gladdens and refreshes and purifies wherever it goes. Jesus calls it "rivers of living water" (John 7:38 KJV).

There is an overflow of love. Sin brings in an overflow of hate, so that the world is filled with wars and murders, slanders, oppression, and selfishness. But this blessing causes love to overflow. Schools, colleges, and hospitals are built. Shelters, rescue homes, and orphanages are opened. Sinners love their own, but this blessing makes us to love all—strangers, the ungodly, and even our enemies.

There is an overflow of peace. It settles old quarrels and grudges. It makes a different atmosphere in the home. The children know it when father and mother get the Comforter. Kindly words and sweet goodwill take the place of bitterness and strife. I suspect that even the dumb beasts realize the overflow.

I heard a humorous story of a man whose cow would switch her tail in his face and then kick over the pail when he was milking her, after which he would always give her a beating with the stool on which he sat. But he got the blessing, and his heart was overflowing with peace. The next morning he went to milk that cow, and when the pail was nearly full, *swish* came the tail in his face, and with a vicious kick she knocked over the pail and then ran across the barnyard. The blessed man picked up the empty pail and stool and went over to the cow, which stood trembling, awaiting the usual kicks and beating. But instead he patted her gently, and said, "You may kick over that pail as often as you please but I am not going to beat you anymore." And the cow seemed to understand, for she dropped her head, quietly began to eat, and never kicked again! That story is good enough to be true, and I don't doubt that it is, for certainly when the Comforter comes a great peace fills the heart and overflows through all the life.

There is an overflow of joy. It makes the face to shine. It glances from the eye and bubbles out in thanksgiving and praise. You never can tell when one who has the blessing will shout out, "Glory to God! Praise the Lord! Hallelujah! Amen!"

I have sometimes seen a whole congregation awakened and refreshed and gladdened by the joyous overflow from one clean-hearted soul. A man or woman with an overflow of genuine joy is worth a whole company of ordinary folks, a host within him- or her-self, and a living proof of the text, "The joy of the LORD is your strength" (Neh. 8:10 NLT).

There is an overflow of patience and long-suffering. A man got this blessing and his wife was so enraged that she left him, went across the way, and lived as the wife of his unmarried brother. He was terribly tempted to take his gun and go over and kill them both. But he prayed about it, and the Lord gave him the patience and long-suffering of Jesus, who bears long with the one who leaves Him and joins with the world. And the man continued to treat them with the utmost kindness, as though they had done him no wrong. Some people might say the man was weak, but I would say he was unusually "strong in the grace that is in Christ Jesus" (2 Tim. 2:1 KJV), and a neighbor of his told me that all his neighbors believed in his faith.

There is an overflow of goodness and generosity. I read the other day of a poor man who supports eight workers in the foreign mission field. When asked how he did it, he replied that he did his own washing, denied himself, and managed his affairs in order to do it.

Do you ask, "How can I get such a blessing?" You will get it by bringing in all the tithes, by giving yourself in love and obedience and wholehearted, joyous consecration to Jesus, as a true bride gives herself to her husband. Do not try to bargain with the Lord and buy it of Him, but wait on Him in never-give-in prayer and confident expectation, and He will give it to you. And then you must not hold it selfishly for your own gratification, but let it overflow to the hungry, thirsty, fainting world about you. God bless you even now and do for you exceeding abundantly above all you ask or think!

One person went from one of my meetings recently with a heart greatly burdened for the blessing, and for two or three days and nights did little else but read the Bible and pray and cry to God for a clean heart filled with the Spirit. At last the Comforter came, and with Him fullness of peace and joy and soul rest, and that day this individual led a number of others into the blessing. "If you then, though you are evil, know how to give good gifts to your children, how much more will your Father in heaven give the Holy Spirit to those who ask him!" (Luke 11:13 NIV). "Ask . . . seek . . . knock" (Matt. 7:7 KJV).

The Key to Spiritual Leadership 22

A mighty man or woman inspires and trains others to be mighty. We wonder and exclaim often at the slaughter of Goliath by David, and we forget that David was the forerunner of a race of fearless, invincible warriors and giant killers. If we would only study and remember the story of David's mighty men in this light, it would be most instructive to us.

Moses inspired a tribe of cowering, toiling, sweaty, grimy, spiritless slaves to lift up their heads, straighten their backs, and throw off the yoke, and he led them forth with songs of victory and shouts of triumph from under the iron bondage of Pharaoh. He fired them with a national spirit and welded and organized them into a distinct and compact people that could be hurled with irresistible power against the walled cities and trained warriors of Canaan.

But what was the secret of David and Moses? David was only a stripling shepherd boy when he immortalized himself. What was his secret? To be sure, Moses was "learned in all the wisdom of the Egyptians" (Acts 7:22 ESV) and doubtless had been trained in all the civil, military, and scientific learning of his day, but he was so weak in himself that he feared and fled at the first word of questioning and disparagement that he heard (see Ex. 2:14) and spent the next forty years feeding sheep for another man in the rugged wilderness of Sinai.

What, then, was their secret? Doubtless, they were cast in a finer mold than most, but their secret was not in themselves.

Joseph Parker declared that great lives are built on great promises, and so they are. These men had so far humbled themselves that they found God. They got close to Him, and He spoke to them. He gave them promises. He revealed His way and truth to them, and as they trusted Him—believing His promises and fashioning their lives according to His truth, His doctrine—everything else followed. They became workers together with God (see 2 Cor. 6:1), heroes of faith, leaders of others, builders of empire, and, in an important sense, saviors of humanity.

Their secret is an open one. It is the secret of every truly successful spiritual leader from then till now, and there is no other way to success in spiritual leadership.

- They had an experience. They knew God.
- This experience, this acquaintance with God, was maintained and deepened and broadened in obedience to God's teaching, or truth, or doctrine.

- They patiently yet urgently taught others what they themselves had learned, and declared, so far as they saw it, the whole counsel of God.

They were abreast of the deepest experiences and fullest revelations God had yet made to humanity. They were leaders, not laggards. They were not in the rear of the procession of God's warriors and saints; they were in the forefront.

Here we discover the importance of the doctrine and experience of holiness through the baptism of the Holy Spirit to leaders. We are to know God and glorify Him and reveal Him to others. We are to finish the work of Jesus, and "fill up . . . what is lacking in the afflictions of Christ" (Col. 1:24 NKJV). We are to rescue the slaves of sin, to make a people, to fashion them into a holy nation, and to inspire and lead them forth to save the world. How can we do this? Only by being in the forefront of God's spiritual hosts—not in name and in titles only, but in reality—by being in glad possession of the deepest experiences God gives, and the fullest revelations He makes to humanity.

The astonishing military and naval successes of the Japanese are said to be due to their profound study, clear understanding, and firm grasp of the theory—the principles, the doctrines—of war; their careful and minute preparation of every detail of their campaigns; the scientific accuracy and precision with which they carry out all their plans; and their utter personal devotion to their cause.

Our war is far more complex and desperate than theirs, its issues are infinitely more far-reaching, and we must equip ourselves for it. And nothing is so vital to our cause as a mastery of the *doctrine* and an assured and joyous possession of the Pentecostal *experience* of holiness through the indwelling Spirit.

THE DOCTRINE

What is the teaching of God's Word about holiness? If we carefully study God's Word, we find that He wants His people to be holy, and the making of a holy people, after the pattern of Jesus, is the Holy Spirit's crowning work. He commands us to "cleanse ourselves from all filthiness of the flesh and spirit, perfecting holiness in the fear of the Lord" (2 Cor. 7:1 KJV). It is prayed that we may "increase and abound in love to one another and to all . . . so that He may establish [our] hearts blameless in holiness before our God and Father at the coming of our Lord Jesus Christ with all His saints" (1 Thess. 3:12–13 NKJV). He says, "As he who called you is holy, you also be holy in all your conduct, since it is written, 'You shall be holy, for I am holy'" (1 Pet. 1:15–16 ESV). And in the most earnest manner we are exhorted to "pursue peace with all people, and holiness, without which no one will see the Lord" (Heb. 12:14 NKJV).

As we further study the Word, we discover that holiness is more than simple freedom from condemnation for wrongdoing. A helpless invalid lying on a bed of sickness, unable to do anything wrong, may be free from the condemnation of actual wrongdoing, and yet it may be in that person's heart to do all manner of evil. Holiness on its negative side is a state of heart purity; it is heart cleanness—cleanness of thought and temper and disposition, cleanness of intention and purpose and wish—a state of freedom from all sin, both in- and outward (see Rom. 6:18). On the positive side it is a state of union with God in Christ, in which the whole individual becomes a temple of God and filled with the fruit of the Spirit, which is "love, joy, peace, patience, kindness, goodness, faithfulness, gentleness, and self-control" (Gal. 5:22–23 NLT). It is moral and spiritual sympathy and harmony with God in the holiness of His nature.

We must not, however, confuse purity with maturity. Purity is a matter of the heart and is secured by an instantaneous act of the Holy Spirit. Maturity is largely a matter of the head and results from growth in knowledge and experience. In one, the heart is made clean and is filled with love. In the other, the head is gradually corrected and filled with light, and so the heart is enlarged and more firmly established in faith; consequently, the experience deepens and becomes stronger and more robust in every way. It is for this reason that we need teachers after we are sanctified, and to this end we are exhorted to humbleness of mind.

My little boy—with a heart full of sympathy and love for his father—may voluntarily go into the garden to weed the vegetables. But, being yet unlearned, lacking light in his head, he pulls up my sweet corn with the grass and weeds. His little heart glows with pleasure and pride in the thought that he is helping Papa, and yet he is doing the very thing I don't want him to do. But if I am a wise and patient father, I will be pleased with him, for what is the loss of a few stalks of corn compared to the expression and development of his love and loyalty? And I shall commend him for the love and faithful purpose of his little heart, while I patiently set to work to enlighten the darkness of his little head. His heart is pure toward his father, but he is not yet mature. In this matter of light and maturity, holy people often widely differ, and this causes much perplexity and needless and unwise anxiety. In the fourteenth chapter of Romans, Paul discussed and illustrated the principle underlying this distinction between purity and maturity.

As we continue to study the Word under the illumination of the Spirit, who is given to lead us into all truth, we further learn that holiness is not a state we reach in experiencing salvation. The apostles had forsaken all to follow Jesus (see Matt. 19:27–29). Their names were written in heaven (see Luke 10:20). Yet they were not holy. They doubted and feared, and were rebuked again and again for the slowness and littleness of their faith. They were bigoted and wanted to call down fire from heaven to consume those who would not receive Jesus (see Luke 9:51–56). They were frequently contending among themselves as to who should be the greatest, and when the supreme test came they all forsook Jesus and fled. Certainly, they were not only afflicted with darkness in their heads but—far worse—carnality in their hearts. They were His, and they were very dear to Him, but they were not yet holy; they were still impure of heart.

Paul made this point very clear in his epistle to the Corinthians. He told them plainly that they were yet only babes in Christ, because they were carnal and contentious (see 1 Cor. 3:1). They were followers of Jesus, they were in Christ, but they were not holy.

It is of great importance that we keep this truth well in mind that people may truly have entered into new life, may be babes in Christ, and yet not be pure in heart. We shall then sympathize more fully with them and see more clearly how to help them and guide their feet into the way of holiness and peace.

Those who hold that we are sanctified wholly when we experience salvation will meet with much to perplex them in their converts and are not intelligently equipped to bless and help God's little children.

A continued study of God's teaching on this subject will clearly reveal to us that purity of heart is obtained after we experience new life in Christ. Peter made this very plain in his address to the Council of Jerusalem, where he recounted the outpouring of the Holy Spirit upon Cornelius and his household. After mentioning the gift of the Holy Spirit, he added, "And put no difference between us and them, purifying their hearts by faith" (Acts 15:9 KJV). Among other things, then, the baptism of the Holy Spirit purifies the heart. But the disciples were converted before they received this Pentecostal experience, so we see that heart purity, or holiness, is a work performed in us after conversion.

Again, we notice that Peter said, "Purifying their hearts by faith." If it is by faith, then it is not by growth, nor by works, nor by death, nor by purgatory after death. It is God's work. He purifies the heart, and He does it for those—and only those—who, devoting all their possessions and powers to Him, seek Him by simple, prayerful, obedient, expectant, unwavering faith through His Son our Savior.

Unless we grasp these truths and hold them firmly, we shall not be able to rightly divide the Word of Truth and so shall hardly be "approved to God, a worker who does not need to be ashamed" (2 Tim. 2:15 NKJV). Someone has written that "the searcher in science knows that if he but stumble in his hypotheses—that if he but let himself be betrayed into prejudices or undue leaning toward pet theory, or anything but absolute uprightness of mind—his whole work will be stultified, and he will fail ignominiously. To get anywhere in science he must follow truth with absolute rectitude."[1]

And is there not a science of salvation, of holiness, of eternal life, that requires the same absolute loyalty to "the Spirit of truth" (John 16:13 KJV)? How infinitely important, then, that we know what that truth is, that we may understand and hold that doctrine.

A friend of mine, who some time ago finished his course with joy and was called into the presence of his Lord to receive his crown, has pointed out some mistakes we must carefully avoid:

It is a great mistake to substitute repentance for Bible consecration.

The people whom Paul exhorted to full sanctification were those who had "turned from their idols to serve the living and true God," and to wait for His Son from heaven.

Only people who are citizens of His kingdom can claim His sanctifying power. Those who still have idols to renounce may be candidates for conversion, but not for the baptism with the Holy Ghost and fire.

It is a mistake in consecration to suppose that the person making it has anything of his own to give. We are not our own, but we are bought with a price, and entire sanctification is simply taking our hands off from God's property. To willfully withhold anything from God is to be a God-robber.

It is a mistake to substitute a mere mental assent to God's proprietorship and right to all we have, while withholding complete devotion to Him.

This is theoretical consecration—a rock on which we fear multitudes are being wrecked.

Consecration which does not embrace the crucifixion of self and the funeral of all false ambitions is not the kind which will bring the holy fire.

A consecration is imperfect which does not embrace the speaking faculty [the tongue] and the believing faculty [the heart]; the imagination; and every power of mind, soul, and body, and give all absolutely and forever into the hands of Jesus, turning a deaf ear to every opposing voice.

Reader, have you made such a consecration? . . . It must embrace all of this, or it will prove a bed of quicksand to sink your soul, instead of a full salvation balloon, which will safely bear you above the fog and malaria and turmoil of the world, where you can triumphantly sing: "I rise to float in realms of light, above the world and sin, with heart made pure and garments white, and Christ enthroned within."

It is a mistake to teach seekers for entire sanctification to "only believe," without complete abandonment to God at every point; for they can no more do it than an anchored ship can sail.

It is a mistake to substitute mere verbal assent for obedient trust. "Only believe" is a fatal snare to all who fall into [these] traps.

It is a mistake to believe that the altar sanctifies the gift without the assurance that all is on the altar. If even the end of your tongue, or one cent of your money, or a straw's weight of false ambition, or spirit of dictation, or one ounce of your reputation or will or believing powers be left off the altar, you can no more believe than a bird without wings can fly.

"Only believe" is only for those seekers of holiness who are truly converted, fully consecrated, and completely crucified to everything but the whole will of God. For these, and these only.

Teachers who apply it to people who have not yet reached the stations named should be taught. All who have reached them may lift up their hands in faith, and look God in the face, and triumphantly sing: "The blood, the blood is all my plea, Hallelujah, for it cleanseth me."[2]

THE EXPERIENCE

Simply to be skilled in the doctrine is not sufficient for us as leaders. We may be as orthodox as Paul himself and yet be as "sounding brass, or a clanging cymbal" (1 Cor. 13:1 NKJV) unless we are rooted in the blessed experience of holiness. If we would save ourselves and those who follow us, if we would make havoc of the Devil's kingdom and build up God's kingdom, we must not only know and preach the truth, but we must be living examples of the saving and sanctifying power of the truth. We are to be living epistles, "known and read by all" (2 Cor. 3:2 ESV). We must be able to say with Paul, "Follow me as I follow Christ" (see 1 Cor. 11:1) and, "Whatever you have learned or received or heard from me, or seen in me—put it into practice. And the God of peace will be with you" (Phil. 4:9 NIV).

We must not forget that we are ourselves simple Christians, individual souls struggling for eternal life and liberty, and we must by all means save ourselves. To this end we must be holy, or else we shall at last experience the awful woe of those who, having preached to others, are yet castaways themselves (see 1 Cor. 9:27).

We also must not forget that we are leaders upon whom multitudes depend. It is a joy and honor to be a leader, but it is also a grave responsibility. James said we "will be judged more strictly" (James 3:1 NLT). How inexpressible shall be our blessedness and how vast our reward if, wise in the doctrine and rich and strong and clean in the experience of holiness, we lead our people into their full heritage in Jesus! But how terrible shall be our condemnation and how great our loss if, in spiritual slothfulness and unbelief, we stop short of the experience ourselves and leave them to perish for want of the gushing waters and heavenly food and divine direction we should have brought them! We need the experience for ourselves, and we need it for our work and for our people.

What the roof is to a house, the doctrine is to our system of truth. It completes it. What sound and robust health is to our bodies, the experience is to our souls. It makes us every whit whole and fits us for all duty. Sweep away the doctrine, and the experience will soon be lost. Lose the experience, and the doctrine will surely be neglected, if not attacked and denied. No one can have the heart—even if he or she has the head—to fully and faithfully and constantly preach the doctrine without the experience.

Spiritual things are spiritually discerned, and as this doctrine deals with the deepest things of the Spirit, it is clearly understood and best recommended, explained, defended, and enforced only by those who have the experience.

Without the experience, the presentation of the doctrine will be faulty and cold and lifeless, or weak and vacillating, or harsh and sharp and severe. With the experience, the preaching of the doctrine will be with great joy and assurance, and will be strong and searching, but at the same time warm and persuasive and tender.

I shall never forget the shock of mingled surprise and amusement and grief with which I heard a Salvation Army captain loudly announce in one of my meetings many years ago that he was "going to preach holiness now" and his people "have to get it" if he had to "ram it down their throats." Poor fellow! He did not possess the experience himself, and never pressed into it, and soon forsook his people.

Anyone with a clear experience of the blessing will never think of "ramming" it down people but will—with much secret prayer, constant meditation and study, patient instruction, faithful warning, loving persuasion, and burning, joyful testimony—seek to lead them into that entire and glad consecration and that fullness of faith that never fails to receive the blessing.

Again, the most accurate and complete knowledge of the doctrine, and the fullest possession of the experience, will fail us at last unless we carefully guard ourselves at several points, and unless we watch and pray.

We must not judge ourselves so much by our feelings as by our volitions. It is not my feelings, but the purpose of my heart, the attitude of my will, that God looks at, and it is to that I must look. "If our heart condemn us not, then have we confidence toward God" (1 John 3:21 KJV). A friend of mine who had firmly grasped this thought and walked continually with God used to testify, "I am just as good when I don't feel good as when I do feel good." Another mighty man of God said that all the feeling he needed to enable him to trust God was the consciousness that he was fully submitted to all the known will of God.

We must not forget that the Devil is "the accuser of our brothers and sisters" (Rev. 12:10 NLT), and that he seeks to turn our eyes away from Jesus—who is our Surety and our Advocate—to ourselves, our feelings, our infirmities, our failures. And if he succeeds in this, gloom will fill us, doubts and fears will spring up within us, and we shall soon fail and fall. We must be wise as the conies and build our nest in the cleft of the Rock of Ages.

We must not divorce conduct from character or works from faith. Our lives must square with our teaching. We must live what we preach. We must not suppose that faith in Jesus excuses us from patient, faithful, laborious service. We must live "by every word that comes from the mouth of God" (Matt. 4:4 NLT). That is, we must fashion our lives, our conduct, our conversation by the principles laid down in His Word, remembering His searching saying, "Not everyone who says to me, 'Lord, Lord,' will enter the kingdom of heaven, but only the one who does the will of my Father who is in heaven" (Matt. 7:21 NIV).

This subject of faith and works is very fully discussed by James (see James 2:14–26), and Paul was very clear in his teaching that, while God saves us not by our works but by His mercy through faith, yet we may "devote [our]selves to doing what is good" (Titus 3:14 NIV) and, "We are God's handiwork, created in Christ Jesus to do good works, which God prepared in advance for us to do" (Eph. 2:10 NIV). Faith must work through love (see Gal. 5:6), emotion must be transmitted into action; joy must lead to work; and love must be turned into faithful, self-sacrificing service, or else they become a kind of pleasant and respectable—but nonetheless deadly—debauchery, and at last ruin us.

However blessed and satisfactory our present experience may be, we must not rest in it, but remember that our Lord has yet many things to say to us, as we are able to receive them. We must stir up the gift of God that is in us, and say with Paul, "One thing I do, forgetting those things which are behind, and reaching forth [like a runner] unto those things which are before, I press toward the mark for the prize of the high calling of God in Christ Jesus" (Phil. 3:13–14 KJV). It is at this point that many fail. They seek the Lord, they weep and struggle and pray, and then they believe—but instead of pressing on, they sit down to enjoy the blessing, and then it escapes them. The children of Israel had to follow the pillar of cloud and fire. It made no difference when it moved. By day or by night, they followed. And when the Comforter comes we must follow, if we would abide in Him and be filled with all the fullness of God. And, oh, the joy of following Him!

Finally, if we have the blessing—not the harsh, narrow, unprogressive exclusiveness which often calls itself by the sweet, heavenly term of *holiness*, but the vigorous, courageous, self-sacrificing, tender, Pentecostal experience of perfect love—we shall both save ourselves and enlighten the world. Our converts will be strong, our candidates for ministry will multiply, and will be able, daredevil men and women. And our people will come to be like the brethren of Gideon, of whom it was said, "each one resembled the children of a king" (Judg. 8:18 KJV).

NOTES

1. John Brisben Walker, "What Is Education? The Studies Most Important for the Modern Man," *The Cosmopolitan Magazine*, vol. 37, August 1904.

2. M. W. Knapp, quoted in Aaron Merritt Hills, *A Hero of Faith and Prayer; Or, Life of Rev. Martin Wells Knapp* (Cincinnati: Mount of Blessings, 1902), 151–153.

Victory over Evil Temper 23

Two letters recently reached me (one from Oregon and one from Massachusetts) inquiring if I thought it possible to have temper destroyed. The person from Oregon wrote, "I have been wondering if the statement is correct when one says, 'My temper is all taken away.' Do you think the temper is destroyed or sanctified? It seems to me that if one's temper were actually gone [one] would not be good for anything."

The person from Massachusetts wrote, "Two of our young people have had the question put to them: 'Is it possible to have all temper taken out of our hearts?' One claims it is possible. The other holds that the temper is not taken out, but God gives power to overcome it." Evidently these are questions that perplex many people, and yet the answer seems simple to me.

Temper, in the sense in which the word is generally used, is not a faculty or power of the soul, but is rather an irregular, passionate, violent expression of selfishness. When selfishness is destroyed by love, by the incoming of the Holy Spirit—revealing Jesus to us as an uttermost Savior and creating within us a clean heart—of course such evil temper is gone, just as the friction and consequent wear and heat of two wheels is gone when the cogs are perfectly adjusted to each other. The wheels are far better off without friction, and just so we are far better off without such temper.

We do not destroy the wheels to get rid of the friction, but we readjust them. That is, we put them into right relations with each other, and then they do their work noiselessly and perfectly. So, strictly speaking, sanctification does not destroy self, but it destroys selfishness— the abnormal and mean and disordered manifestation and assertion of self. I myself am to be sanctified, rectified, purified, brought into harmony with God's will as revealed in His Word, and united to Him in Jesus, so that His life of holiness and love flows continually through all the avenues of my being, as the sap of the vine flows through all parts of the branch. "I am the vine; you are the branches," said Jesus (John 15:5 NLT).

When people are thus filled with the Holy Spirit, they are not turned into putty or made into jellyfish, with all powers of resistance taken out. They do not have any less force and "push" and "go" than before, but rather more, for all natural energy is now reinforced by the Holy Spirit and turned into channels of love and peace instead of hate and strife.

They may still feel indignation in the presence of wrong, but it will not be rash, violent, explosive, and selfish, as before they were sanctified, but calm, orderly, holy, and determined, like that of God. It will be the wholesome, natural antagonism of holiness and righteousness to all unrighteousness and evil.

Such people will feel it when they are wronged, but it will be much in the same way that they feel when others are wronged. The personal, selfish element will be absent. At the same time there will be pity and compassion and yearning love for the wrongdoer and a greater desire to see that person saved than to see him or her punished.

A sanctified man was walking down the street the other day with his wife when a filthy fellow on a passing wagon insulted her with foul words. Instantly the temptation came to the man to want to get hold of him and punish him, but just as quickly the indwelling Comforter whispered, "If you forgive those who sin against you" (Matt. 6:14 NLT), and instantly the clean heart of the man responded, "I will, I do forgive him, Lord." Then, instead of anger a great love filled his soul, and instead of hurling a brick or hot words at the poor Devil-deceived fellow, he sent a prayer to God in heaven for him. There was no friction in his soul. He was perfectly adjusted to his Lord. His heart was perfectly responsive to his Master's word, and he could rightly say, "My temper is gone." We must have our spiritual eyes wide open to discern the difference between sinful temper and righteous indignation.

Many people wrong and rob themselves by calling their fits of temper "righteous indignation." On the other hand, there is here and there a timid soul who is so afraid of sinning through temper as to suppress the wholesome antagonism that righteousness, to be healthy and perfect, must express toward all unrighteousness and sin.

It takes the keen-edged Word of God, applied by the Holy Spirit, to cut away unholy temper without destroying righteous antagonism, to enable us to hate and fight sin with spiritual weapons (see 2 Cor. 10:3–5) while pitying and loving the sinner, to so fill us with the mind of Jesus that we will feel as badly over a wrong done to a stranger as though it were done to us, and to help us put away the personal feeling and be as calm and unselfish and judicial in opposing wrong as is the judge upon the bench. Into this state of heart and mind we who are entirely sanctified by the indwelling Holy Spirit are brought.

Dr. Asa Mahan, Finney's friend and coworker, had a quick and violent temper in his youth and young manhood. But one day he believed, God sanctified him, and for fifty years he said he never felt but one uprising of temper, and that was but for an instant, about five years after he received the blessing. For the following forty-five years, though subjected to many trials and provocations, he felt only love and peace and patience and goodwill in his heart.

A Christian woman was confined to her bed for years with nervous and other troubles, and was very cross and touchy and petulant. At last she became convinced that the Lord had a better experience for her, and she began to pray for a clean heart full of patient, holy, humble love. She prayed so earnestly, so violently, that her family became alarmed lest she should wear out her poor, frail body in her struggle for spiritual freedom. But she told them she was determined to have the blessing, if it cost her life, and so she continued to pray, until one glad, sweet day the Comforter came. Her heart was purified, and from that day forth, in spite of the fact that she was still a nervous invalid, suffering constant pain, she never showed the least sign of temper or impatience, but was full of meekness and patient, joyous thankfulness.

Love took up the harp of Life, and smote on all the
chords with might;
Smote the chord of Self, that, trembling, pass'd
in music out of sight.[1]

Such is the experience of one in whom Jesus lives without a rival
and in whom grace has done its perfect work.

"No form of vice, not worldliness, not greed of gold, not drunk-
enness itself, does more to unchristianize society than evil temper,"[2]
says a distinguished and thoughtful writer. If this is true, it must be
God's will that we be saved from it. And it is provided for in the
uttermost salvation that Jesus offers.

Do you want this blessing? If so, be sure of this: God has not
begotten such a desire in your heart to mock you; you may have it. God
is able to do even this for you. From a human perspective, it is impossible, but not from God's perspective. Look at Him just now for it. It
is His work, His gift. Look at your past failures and acknowledge
them. Look at your present and future difficulties, count them up and
face them every one, and admit that they are more than you can hope
to conquer, but then look at the dying Son of God, your Savior—the
Man with the seamless robe, the crown of thorns, and the nail-prints.
Look at the fountain of His blood. Look at His Word. Look at the
almighty Holy Spirit, who will dwell within you, if you trust and obey,
and cry out, "It shall be done! The mountain shall become a plain; the
impossible shall become possible!" Quietly, intelligently, abandon yourself to the Holy Spirit right now in simple, glad, obedient faith, and the
blessing shall be yours.

NOTES

1. Alfred Lord Tennyson, "Locksley Hall," 1835, public domain.

2. Henry Drummond, *The Greatest Thing in the World*, rev. ed. (Grand Rapids, MI: Revell, 2011), 30.

Samuel L. Brengle's Holy Life Series

This series comprises the complete works of Samuel L. Brengle, combining all nine of his original books into six volumes, penned by one of the great minds on holiness. Each volume has been lovingly edited for modern readership by popular author (and long-time Brengle devotee) Bob Hostetler. Brengle's authentic voice remains strong, now able to more relevantly engage today's disciples of holiness. These books are must-haves for all who would seriously pursue and understand the depths of holiness in the tradition of John Wesley.

Helps to Holiness
ISBN: 978-1-63257-064-2
eBook: 978-1-63257-065-9

The Heart of Holiness
ISBN: 978-1-63257-066-6
eBook: 978-1-63257-067-3

The Servant's Heart
ISBN: 978-1-63257-068-0
eBook: 978-1-63257-069-7

Ancient Prophets and Modern Problems
ISBN: 978-1-63257-070-3
eBook: 978-1-63257-071-0

Come Holy Guest
ISBN: 978-1-63257-072-7
eBook: 978-1-63257-073-4

Resurrection Life and Power
ISBN: 978-1-63257-074-1
eBook: 978-1-63257-075-8

**Samuel L. Brengle's
Holy Life Series Box Set**
ISBN: 978-1-63257-076-5